featherweight BOATBUILDING

featherweight BOATBUILDING

a WoodenBoat book by
"Mac" McCarthy

FOR YOUR SAFETY
Working in a boatshop requires certain consid-
erations to ensure your safety and health. We want
you to enjoy doing your own work, but urge you to
exercise caution throughout the process. Before using
a power or hand tool with which you are unfamiliar,
consult operating instructions. Many materials found
in boatshops are deadly and have long-term ill effects;
before using any toxic material, consult the Material
Safety Data Sheet for that substance. Above all, protect yourself from improper use that may lead to permanent injury or death.

Copyright 1996 by Henry McCarthy
Second printing 1997

Book design by Nina Kennedy
Cover design by Richard Gorski
Peter H. Spectre, Editor
Patricia J. Lown, Proofreader
Photographs, unless otherwise noted,
by Gary Crowell and Mac McCarthy
Printed in the United States of America
Cover photographs by Rich Hilsinger
A WoodenBoat Book
ISBN 0-937822-39-6

DEDICATION
To Alice, for helping me pursue my dream

ACKNOWLEDGEMENTS:
Thanks to Jon Wilson and the staff
at *WoodenBoat* magazine and
WoodenBoat School for giving me the
opportunity to teach my chosen craft.

Thanks to Peter H. Spectre for
his support through the years and for
his editorial support in the writing
of this book.

Thanks to my students, who have
taught me so much.

Contents

featherweight
BOATBUILDING

INTRODUCTION

Have you ever wished you could have a really hand-some boat? One that you could build yourself in a reasonable period of time? A boat that would be worth far more than the price of the materials to build it? A boat that would be admired by anyone who saw it for its elegance and grace? A boat that would be both lightweight and strong?

This book will show you how to build just such a boat by the strip-planking method, using cedar as the principal planking stock. The techniques you will learn here can be used to build a wide variety of small boats.

One of the main reasons I use the cedar-strip system of boatbuilding is that it is versatile. It has allowed me to build canoes, recreational rowing shells, sea kayaks, and other small craft for years with excellent results. The system is also perfect for building lightweight catamarans and trimarans, and for constructing iceboat masts. I am convinced that this is the easiest system available to the amateur for building elegant small craft at a reasonable price.

There seems to be a trend these days towards quick-and-dirty boatbuilding, which emphasizes box-like shapes in plywood that can be knocked together by an inexperienced builder in a weekend. Boats like this are a way to get started, but I feel most people will be disappointed with the result of their efforts.

I feel very strongly that a boat should be elegant looking as well as functional, and for that reason I suggest that anyone new to small-craft construction start with a classy little double-paddle

Peaceful, engrossing, satisfying — featherweight boatbuilding elevates you from the tensions of everyday life.

you need to know to build another type of boat, perhaps more complex, if you should so desire.

The system we will use to build the Wee Lassie does not require any steam-bending or intricate machining of parts. It does require a few hand tools, and several inexpensive power tools. Here's an overview of the construction method:

A simple building board is made on which to erect molds cut with the aid of patterns. For the Wee Lassie, nine molds are enough to create the shape of the finished boat. These molds do not remain in the boat; rather, they are removed after the hull is planked. Around these molds we bend strips from end to end, temporarily fastening them to the molds, while edge gluing them to each other with carpenter's glue.

When the glue has set, we plane and sand the hull smooth, and then seal the wood with epoxy. The boat is then covered with four-ounce fiberglass cloth set in epoxy resin. When wet out with epoxy the fiberglass cloth turns transparent and the wood shows through with all its grain and pretty color enriched in the process.

After it has been coated, the hull is removed from the molds, and the inside is sanded and then also coated with fiberglass and epoxy. Rails, a thwart, seat stringers, and decks are added. Air chambers for extra flotation can also built at one or both ends if desired. The hull is then finish-sanded and varnished. Finally, a double paddle is made, and the seat is framed and then caned.

canoe. My personal favorite, for many reasons, is the Wee Lassie. It is small enough to be built in limited space, it doesn't require a major investment in materials, and the amount of work involved is not enough to make what should be fun into a chore. Building the Wee Lassie allows you to experience the satisfaction of building something really nice with your own two hands and teaches you all the techniques

Because of the nature of wood, each Wee Lassie is unique in color and wood-grain pattern, but all are good looking. The fanciness of the appearance and the quality of the finish are up to the individual builder. A thwart, for example, can be a simple, straight piece of wood with the edges rounded off, or it can be a complexly carved or shaped sculpture.

Some builders will apply three coats of varnish to their canoes and be perfectly satisfied with the results; others will use ten coats and wet sand between them until the boats gleam like multifaceted gems. On my own boats — and I have built a lot of them — I try for a happy medium between perfection and common sense. I want a

Two featherweight double-paddle canoes, ready for a voyage along a quiet backwater.

good-looking boat, but I also want to be able to paddle it without worrying about scratching a glass-like finish I may have spent hours to achieve.

Building a featherweight canoe is not instant boatbuilding. You don't slap a few pieces of plywood together one day and launch the boat the next. You can expect to spend over a hundred hours on this little craft, but it will be time well spent. Not only will you have the satisfaction of creating something worthwhile, but also you will have years of pleasure in using the little boat.

The original Wee Lassie, an undecked double-paddle canoe, was created in the late 1800s in upper New York State by a canoe builder named J. Henry Rushton. Most of the double-paddle canoes in Rushton's era were like the present sea kayak: they had full decks but were wider in beam for more stability. They were not designed to be Eskimo rolled; rather, they were intended to be paddled easily in an upright position. The Wee Lassie type of canoe differed from its contemporaries by being open — that is, undecked — thus saving a lot of weight.

This is not Charles Atlas, and this is not a stunt. This is a normal person with a normal featherweight canoe.

What could be simpler? A paddle, a backrest, a seat cushion, and a parka in the event of rain. This is my own canoe.

Without cutting any corners, a Wee Lassie that weighs just a little over twenty pounds can be built using the methods described in this book. (The boat can be built to be even lighter, but we want an elegant canoe, not a fragile one.) Because of this light weight, these little boats are a delight to paddle and are easy for one person to carry. You sit on a comfortable seat, with a thwart for a backrest, and a foot brace to enhance your paddling ability. You also sit low in the boat, which provides excellent stability. I almost always carry a camera and binoculars with me when I paddle, and the last thing I want to do is practice swimming.

The only time I have been dumped in a Wee Lassie was while playing in surf, and I therefore don't recommend an open boat for that. The canoe paddles well in rough water, but that, of course, depends on the skill of the paddler and the use of common sense. Any small boat does well to stay close inshore.

I paddle my own Wee Lassie all up and down the East Coast of the U.S., on ponds, lakes, rivers, streams and bays, salt water or fresh. I have never felt threatened, but I do try to stay within the limits of my abilities. Open water has little fascination for me. To paddle all day across open water from one island to another, or to an island a long distance from the shore, may be a test of strength, endurance, and navigation skills, but it would be boring to me. I much prefer to paddle along the shoreline of a pond, or up a narrow, twisting estuary or stream. This is where the ibis, egret, and great blue heron fish. This is where the otters play,

This is me in my own Wee Lassie in the Okefenokee Swamp on a break from boatbuilding.

Paddling a Wee Lassie is a quality way to explore a world most people do not even know exists. Within sight of busy highways, high-rise buildings, and luxury condominiums, there are little secret places where you can be quiet and serene, and cruise along a wild shore enjoying your own little world.

You don't have to wait for a two-week vacation or a weekend to enjoy paddling a Wee Lassie. Even near a big city, good paddling can be found only minutes away with a Wee Lassie on top of your car. As an escape from stress and tension, paddling a Wee Lassie can't be beat.

Here in Sarasota, Florida, where I live, there is a small creek that empties into the bay. Paddling up this creek, which most people consider only a drainage ditch, can be fascinating. You are paddling through an old section of town; some of the homes are dilapidated, some are very well kept. Hundred-year-old oak trees shade the narrow stream. The quantity of wildlife is surprising. Egrets, herons, and river otters have adapted to life on the edge of human civilization. Large mullet swirl the water in front of your canoe. Granted, this isn't the same as a voyage in Minnesota's Boundary Waters, but it surely is educational, as well as close to home and available.

and the deer come down to the water's edge to drink.

I enjoy the anticipation of discovery as I round each bend of a stream. I can paddle my Wee Lassie without making a single sound to announce my presence. What will it be? A mother deer and her fawn? An alligator sunning on the bank? A log full of turtles that splash one by one into the water at my approach?

The double-paddle canoe has many advantages over the traditional tandem canoe, which requires two people to carry and handle it effectively. With a featherweight double-paddle canoe, you are master of your own fate. The boat is easily carried by one person, and easily cartopped, so you can go canoeing whenever you want to and with only a few minutes of preparation.

A canoe propelled by a double-bladed paddle is easy to take upstream in shallow water. The experience is like rowing, but you are facing forward. A regular paddle needs two feet of water under the canoe

These students built their Wee Lassies in a course on featherweight boatbuilding I taught at WoodenBoat School in Brooklin, Maine.

No, this Wee Lassie is not floating in air, she's in a clear semi-tropical stream.

only, once the strips and rails are ripped to size.

Throughout this book I will emphasize safety. Any time you use power tools and chemicals, such as a router and epoxy resin, being safety conscious is exercising plain common sense.

I have written this book in an effort to spread the word about a different world that awaits each and every one of you. It is a world without telephones, or fax machines, or television. A world where what you see is real. A world where the boat you explore in has been created by you, the paddle has been uniquely shaped to fit your hands, and even the seat has been woven by you. This is a truly different experience for most people.

Welcome to the world I have lived in for the last fifteen years or so, the world of the featherweight canoe.

to be paddled properly. The double paddle works well in six inches, which is quite a difference. Paddle upstream as far as you want to go, then drift with the current back down to where you started. This is a very pleasant way to go.

Many of the people who come to my shop here in Sarasota, either to visit or to learn how to build a Wee Lassie — I have been teaching boatbuilding for years — have never built anything with their own two hands before. They find that the act of building this boat opens up a whole new world to them even before they use the boat itself. Featherweight boatbuilding has its own pleasures.

The most expensive tools you will need are a table saw, a router, and a random-orbit sander. If you only intend to build one boat, these tools can be rented or borrowed. If time and convenience are not important, you can build one of these boats with hand tools

A Barnegat Bay sneakbox.

A sea kayak.

A few of the many types of elegant boats that can be built with the featherweight boatbuilding method:

A sailing canoe with a simple lateen rig.

A rowing shell with sliding seat and outriggers.

CHAPTER ONE

Getting Started

Building a little boat like the Wee Lassie can be a gratifying experience, made even more enriching if you treat the materials and tools involved in the project with care and respect. Not only does building this little boat entail learning some basic woodworking skills, it also involves learning how to properly sharpen chisels and plane irons, adjust a plane, make your own tools for a specific job, and use epoxies for bonding and as a clear coating. Just as importantly, it includes learning and observing some simple safety rules as you build the boat.

Being careful while you work adds to your enjoyment. Protecting your eyes, lungs, and fingers from injury is usually a simple matter of remaining alert at all times and using a few inexpensive protective devices.

The site you pick to build your boat is important. It should be big enough to allow easy access all around the boat. It should have good ventilation and lighting, and should be protected from the extremes of temperature and the vagaries of weather. The best temperature range would be from 60 to 80 degrees F. Using these criteria, the living room of your home would be ideal, but taking it over to build a boat would probably, perhaps even certainly, cause a divorce. A garage shop is also ideal, providing you can heat it if you will be working in the winter months.

No matter where you choose to work, a good dust-collection system would be a smart investment. If that's not possible, consider a site that will allow you to move any sanding or sawing operations outside; this will keep the heaviest amount of dust out of the shop and will help protect your lungs.

Wood for Strip Planking

My wood of choice for the Wee Lassie is clear Western red cedar. It is light in weight, has interesting color variations, and works well. Other acceptable woods are cypress, redwood, juniper, and Eastern white cedar, but not necessarily in that order. You are looking for the strongest, lightest wood you can find. Using a heavy wood like mahogany for the boat would defeat the purpose in building a featherweight canoe. Even if I could get unlimited mahogany for nothing I would not use it for the entire hull, though if I could get enough sassafras some day to build a Wee Lassie, I would use it. I recently saw a lapstrake sailboat built with this wood, and it was gorgeous.

A trip to the local lumberyard can be intimidating to the first-time builder. Use your telephone to find out if any of the local yards have Western red cedar. If they say yes, ask if they have grade D or better (relatively knot free; only small, tight knots allowed), S4S (surfaced, or planed, on the sides and the edges). If they have it, go get it. You want the equivalent of three 1-inch by 8-inch boards. (Remember that a 1-inch board in lumberyard measure is actually ³/₄-inch thick.) You want flat grain showing on the face of these boards, so you will have edge grain showing after you rip them into strips. (See Figure 1-1.) You will probably have to accept boards with some knots, but try to not pick any boards with small knots spaced out across the board. This would spoil too many strips for our purpose. You are bound to get waste no matter how good the lumber is, but some of the odd pieces can be used on decks, etc.

Explain to the yardman why you need nearly perfect lumber. Show him a photograph from this book if nothing else. Once he sees the quality of the project he may become enthusiastic and helpful, but you may have to pay a premium for the privilege of selecting out the top of the grade.

If you go through a stack of lumber, picking out only a few pieces, make sure you handle the wood gently and replace it as it was. Treat the lumber pile like a campsite; don't trash it for the next person.

If you can't find a local source for Western red cedar, there are numerous companies that will supply rough lumber, finished strips, cove and bead strips, or complete kits, and ship the order to you. Having someone else rip the strips and rout a cove and bead on them more than doubles the cost of the wood, but if you are only going to build one boat, that may be the best way to go. Companies that supply lumber and/or finished strips are listed in Appendix C.

Ripping the Strips

I rip strips on a table saw with a thin-kerf blade set to produce strips exactly ¹/₄-inch thick. (Kerf refers to the thickness of the track the sawblade makes through the wood.) I use a finger board to hold the wood tightly against the rip fence. (See Figure 1-2.)

If you plan to build only one boat, your best bet is to use a 7 ¹/₄-inch hollow-ground planer blade. These are readily available at Sears, or local lumberyards. I use a more expensive 7 ¹/₄-inch carbide-tipped thin-kerf blade only because it stays sharp much longer, and I build a lot of boats. If you have a 10-inch saw and use the blade that came with it, you will create too much waste sawdust. The smaller 7 ¹/₄-inch blade is thinner and cuts a narrower kerf in the wood; as a result it wastes a lot less material. The hollow-ground planer blade leaves a very smooth surface, with sharp edges, which will be an advantage later on if you use a router to cove and bead the strips.

When you start ripping strips, check the first four before continuing to make sure that, when held together, they add up to one inch exactly. This test makes any small error very apparent.

The main reason that you must make every effort to cut the strips exactly ¹/₄ inch thick is to enable the cove and bead router bits to cut the strip edges properly. Let me explain:

For the first ten years or so that I built cedar-strip boats I hand beveled the strips with a block plane so they would fit tightly as I edge-glued them over the molds. (There is nothing wrong with this system, but it takes time and requires a certain amount of proficiency in the use of a hand plane.) Any gaps would show up later, when the boat was cartopped and the sunlight beamed through the epoxy. Finally, I turned to coved and beaded strips, which pretty much eliminate the problem.

Cove and Bead

One edge of a coved and beaded strip is rounded, the other is hollowed. (See Figure 1-3.) When the boat is planked, the rounded edge of one strip fits into the hollowed edge of the one next to it, making it much easier for the beginner to turn out a first-class job. Using coved and beaded strips not only increases the glue surface, but almost automatically fairs the hull as you go along, making clean up and the final sanding process much easier.

To cove and bead your own strips requires a router rigged in a router table with a fence and finger boards, and a set of cove and bead router bits. (See Figure 1-4.) Suppliers for the bits are listed in Appendix C. Prices

range from about $35 to $95, depending on quality. The cheaper bits come from Taiwan, and I recommend them only if you are going to build just one, or at most, a few boats. For heavier production work I would certainly go with the more expensive bits.

The Optional Feature Strip

If you want to include a fancy feature strip in your canoe — that is, a strip of wood that contrasts with the regular planking stock to add interest to the hull — and such a strip does look neat, you should order this at the same time you order the strips or kit. If you are ripping your own strips, you should rip some light-colored strips (I use spruce) to combine with the darkest strips of Western red cedar that you can find. Or, for a plain feature strip you can just run a simple light-colored strip. I usually run my feature strip as the fourth strip down from the sheer. Use your imagination or copy a design from one of the boats shown in this book if you want. (See Figure 1-5.) But do be careful about using an exotic hardwood strip as decoration. It is difficult to get an even surface when sanding hardwood that is next to softwood, so try

Figure 1-1: Clear Western red cedar ready to be ripped into planking strips. The planks have flat grain on the surface; they will be ripped into ¼-inch strips, ¾-inch wide, with vertical grain.

Figure 1-2: Ripping the strips on a table saw. A feather-or finger-board has been clamped to the table to hold the wood securely against the fence.

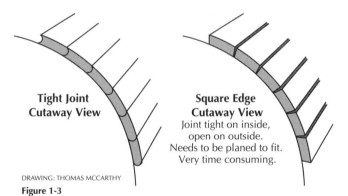

**Tight Joint
Cutaway View**

**Square Edge
Cutaway View**
Joint tight on inside,
open on outside.
Needs to be planed to fit.
Very time consuming.

DRAWING: THOMAS MCCARTHY

Figure 1-3

Figure 1-4: A table-mounted router rigged to cut coved and beaded strips. A fence for guiding the strips is clamped to the table. Four feather- or finger-boards are used — two to hold the strips down and two to hold the strips against the fence. An alternative to this setup would be to job out the coving and beading of the strips.

Figure 1-5: A rather complex feature strip created by sandwiching darker and lighter woods.

to keep the woods you use in the hull similar in hardness.

One way to create a feature strip is to glue a dark strip between two light-colored strips, or vice versa. Clamp the setup and let it cure overnight. (See Figure 1-6.) Clean up one edge of the composite with a plane in the morning, and then run it through the table saw to create two $1/4$-inch by $3/4$-inch strips. These can then be coved and beaded along with the other strips, and used as feature strips.

Recently, I have started using fancier feature strips that involve the use of a cut-off saw to make small blocks that are sandwiched between two light-colored strips and then ripped into two $1/4$-inch by $3/4$-inch strips as above. As you can see, the only limit to feature-strip design is your imagination and patience.

If you plan to build more than one boat, and to rip and rout your own strips, it pays to buy a router with an easily reached knob for micro-adjustments. Most of the big plunge-routers are now equipped with these knobs. They are well worth the extra expense, as the ability to make tiny adjustments saves endless aggravation.

The Molds

Before we can actually start building our boat, we must create and trace the full-sized patterns of the molds onto plywood or particle board and cut them out. We will be planking around those molds after they have been mounted on the building board.

Before we make the molds we have to decide whether we want to build our canoe in the traditional way, using small nails and staples to hold the strips in place while the glue dries; or the way I now build all my custom boats, using clamps, rather than temporary fasteners that leave marks on the finished hull.

Using clamps results in an almost flawless hull but increases the time required to plank the hull. It also requires about 20 spring clamps, and many 36-inch lengths of $3/16$-inch shock cord. The traditional way of building, however, only requires a staple gun with $1/4$-inch and $1/2$-inch staples, and four ounces of 1 $1/4$-inch No. 18 wire nails. All of these fastenings are temporary; they must be removed from the hull before it is sanded and will leave behind holes that must be filled. All those filled holes will show up on the finished boat.

If you decide to clamp the strips rather than nail them, you must cut clamping slots in the molds before they are erected on the building board. (See Figure 1-7.) This means a little more work, but the end result, I think, is worth it.

The molds can be made from $1/2$-inch plywood or particle board. The process of tracing and cutting out the molds is the same, whichever material you use. Handling either will be easier if you or the lumberyard rip the full sheets into three 16-inch-wide strips. If you are building a larger boat than the Wee Lassie, you might have to cut the plywood 18 or 20 inches wide. It pays to check your patterns before you cut your material.

In Appendix D are measured drawings that will enable you to make your own full-sized mold patterns for the Wee Lassie. I have included measured drawings rather than a table of offsets, because I think they are more user friendly. If you don't want to take the time to make your own full-sized patterns, they are available from me at $20 per set. (Feather Canoes, 1705 Andrea Pl., Sarasota, FL 34235; telephone 941-355-6736 or 953-7660.)

If you are using my full-size patterns, keep in mind that the mold pattern for the stems — remember, there are two stems: one at the bow and one at the stern — is superimposed over the station molds, so the stem patterns should be traced onto the plywood first. Use carbon paper, or prick through the patterns into the plywood with an ice pick or small nail and connect the tiny holes with a flexible batten.

Once you have transferred the stem molds, you can cut the pattern sheet on the centerline and cut out the pattern for the largest mold. This pattern shows one-half of the mold — the straight line represents the centerline — so mark one side onto the plywood, then flip the pattern and mark the other side. (See Figure 1-8a.) Make sure the centerline is square with the building-board line. Make sure you mark the location of the sheerline. You can now cut out and trace each smaller mold pattern in order, using the same procedure.

I use a sabersaw to cut out the molds once they have been drawn on the plywood or particle board. (See Figure 1-9.) Mine is a Bosch 1587vs, which is expensive but worth every penny. The Bosch provides good blade visibility, has a blower to keep the area dust free so you can see your line, has a very smooth action, and breaks very few blades. It is an excellent tool. Mine requires a screwdriver to change blades, but newer models have even improved on that.

In my view a tool should be a pleasure to use. It should feel right in your hand, and it should do what it is designed to do without a lot of fuss and bother. There is nothing more aggravating when you are try-

ing to make an accurate cut with a sabersaw than to be distracted by broken blades, a jumpy action, or an unreliable switch. (See Appendix B for specific tool recommendations.)

My experience has been that buying quality tools and taking care of them really pays off in the long run. I have also found that taking the time to build a box for a new tool, its accessories, and the instruction manual extends the life of the tool. I then make it a habit of returning the tool to its box when I am finished with it, instead of putting it down on a sawhorse or bench, where it can easily be knocked off and damaged. The box also serves to protect the tool from dust and grit when it is not being used.

Figure 1-6: Gluing up a feature strip. Plenty of clamps; a layer of plastic to keep the strip from becoming glued to the work surface. Actually, this is a triple-thick strip that will be ripped into two strips, one for each side of the boat.

Figure 1-7: A mold modified with slots for clamping the planking strips. These slots are not necessary if you will be holding the strips in place with temporary nails while the glue sets.

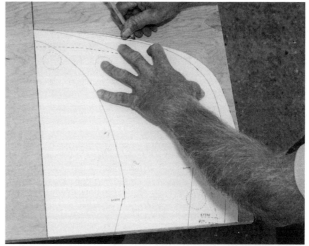

Figure 1-8a: Tracing around a cut-out mold pattern onto the plywood. As this pattern is for one-half of the mold, the pattern must be flipped over to mark the shape of the other side of the mold, as in Figure 1-8b.

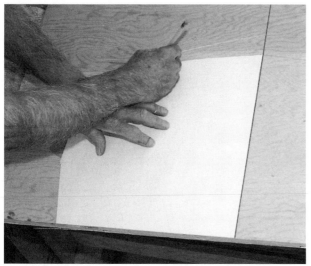

Figure 1-8b: Once this mold has been marked, the pattern sheet will be trimmed to the next smaller mold, and it will be similarly traced.

Figure 1-9: Using a sabersaw to cut out a mold. This mold is for a setup in which the strips will be nailed temporarily in place, so there are no clamping slots.

CHAPTER TWO

Stripping and Sanding the Hull

Before planking can begin, the stems must be prepared to receive the strips. The Wee Lassie has a two-piece stem construction: an inner and an outer stem. The inner stems — one for each end of the boat — are laminated in place on the stem molds; after the hull is planked, the outer stems are laminated over them.

Laminating the Inner Stems

To prepare the stem molds for laminating the stems, drill a series of 1-inch holes in the two stem molds. (See Figure 2-1.) Keep the edge of the holes $\frac{1}{2}$ inch back from the edge of the mold. Nine or ten holes will do. Use masking tape to cover the outer edge of the mold, so your lamination won't stick to the plywood.

For laminating and edge-gluing, I use what is known generically as carpenter's glue, the common yellow type found in most hardware stores. It is inexpensive and does the job very well. It can be sanded off the surface of the wood without leaving permanent stains. It is easy to clean up, and much easier to use than any other suitable glue. Epoxy is much more expensive, is difficult to handle, and requires that you wear gloves at all times. Clean up requires expensive and dangerous solvents. That carpenter's glue is not waterproof is no problem, as the entire hull will later be covered with epoxy, which is.

I experiment with different materials and methods all the time. I do this for my own benefit, and also to pass on practical information in my newsletter. (My newsletter, *The Wee Lassie*, is available for $5 per year from Feather Canoes, 1705 Andrea Pl., Sarasota, FL

34235; 941-355-6736 or 953-7660.) If something is easy to use, reasonably nontoxic, and sensibly priced, I tend to stick with it until something better comes along.

Rip some thin strips of spruce, $^1/_{16}$ inch by $^5/_8$ inch by 32 inches long. When laminating strips around a fairly tight curve, it is better to rip the strips thinner, and use more of them, than to force a thicker strip to the breaking point. Spread carpenter's glue on the strips and, with small C-clamps, laminate these over the stem molds. (See Figure 2-2.) If you don't have enough small C-clamps, you can use small nails to hold the laminations in place. Be sure to pull the nails after the glue has cured or you will have difficulty releasing the molds after the hull has been stripped. Clean up any glue drips, and let the laminations set overnight.

The Building Board

While the glue on the inner stems sets up, we can build and prepare the building board or strongback, the platform on which the molds are erected. The simplest construction is a framework of straight 2 by 4s, 10 feet 9 inches long by 10 inches wide, covered on one side with plywood left over from the molds. (See Figure 2-3.)

The main purpose of the building board is to provide a level surface on which the molds can be anchored. If the building board is twisted, the finished canoe will also be twisted. Sight the building board, and use shims if necessary to take out any twist.

Mount the building board at a convenient working height, between 32 and 36 inches off the floor. You can use sawhorses, or a frame with casters or wheels so you can move the setup around. Being able to move the whole boat outside the shop area for sanding is a real blessing.

A centerline must be struck on the building board. For this I use a piece of nylon seine cord, which is very fine and can be pulled very tight. Put a small nail at the center of each end of the building board, and pull the string taut between the nails. You now have an accurate centerline, and the molds can be erected on the building board.

The plans show the location of the molds and the cleats used to hold the molds in place. Make sure that the cleats, and therefore the molds, are square to the centerline, and fasten them in place. Then fasten the molds to the cleats, making sure the centerlines of the molds align with the centerline of the building board. A battery-operated screw gun makes short work of this operation, but so do a hammer and nails.

If you are working from plans that show the mold spacing only, erect the amidships mold in the indicated position. All molds forward of the amidships mold should be placed so the forward side of the mold is on the station line; all molds aft of the amidships mold should be placed so the after side of the mold is on the station line. This ensures that the strips when laid will hit the edges of the molds exactly at the station lines, and saves having to bevel all the molds.

Now cover the edges of the molds with masking tape to prevent the strips from becoming glued to the molds. Don't forget to do this, or you will have great difficulty getting the stripped hull off the building jig.

Beveling the Stem and Hanging the First Strip

With all the molds erected and checked for alignment, bevel the inner stems to receive the planking. Take a short piece of strip and run it past the first mold and the stem to determine the correct bevel. Then remove the stems from the stem molds and cut the bevel at the bench with a sharp block plane. Remount the stems on the stem molds, holding them in place with a few small C-clamps.

Planking begins at the sheer. Since the boat is being built upside down, you will be planking upward toward the bottom.

Partially drive a nail at the sheer mark of each mold, allowing the nails to stick out far enough for the first strip to rest on while you either clamp or nail the strip in place, depending on which system you are using.

Rest the first strip on the nail you just placed at the sheer mark on the center mold, making sure you have an even overlap at both ends. Turn this strip cove side down, the rounded edge up. Most builders place the strips on the molds with the rounded edge down, because they find it easier to spread glue on the coved side, facing up. I think my way is better, because it allows me to exert downward pressure on each strip without breaking the fragile edges of the cove. A tight hull is more important to me than ease in spreading glue on the first three or four strips.

Ease this first strip down onto the nails at the sheerline at each mold and tack it in place. I use a 1 $^1/_4$-inch, No. 18 headed nail for the first strip on each side no matter which system I will be using — temporary nails or clamps. This type of nail has more holding power than a $^1/_2$-inch staple, and some of the strips on a Wee Lassie require a fair amount of persuasion to be pulled down tightly to the molds. I use blocks of scrap cedar,

⅛ inch by ⅜ inch by 1 inch, as washers under the nail-heads to make later removal of the nails easier. The thin nail leaves only one hole, which is easy to fill later with a cut-in-half toothpick.

These 1 ¼-inch, No. 18 headed nails were once easy to find at most hardware stores, but no longer. If you have trouble finding these nails, drop me a line, and for $5 I'll send you, post-paid, enough for a couple of boats. I had to buy my supply in bulk and consequently have enough to last me another twenty years or so.

Now put the mate to this first strip on the other side of the boat, following the same procedure. (See Figure 2-4.) Sight the pair to be sure you have a nice, fair sheerline with no humps or bumps. Make any necessary adjustments now, before you glue on the second pair of strips.

There are two ways to handle the strips as they come to the stems on either end of the canoe. One is simply to cut them off flush with the outer edge of the inner stem. (See Figure 2-5.) When all the strips are on,

Figure 2-1: The stem mold, here set up on the building board with the forward section molds, is modified with holes along the outside edge to provide purchase for clamping while the inner stem is laminated.

Figure 2-2: The inner stem is laminated by spreading glue on thin strips, which are then bent around the edge of the mold and clamped until the glue cures. Masking tape is first applied to the face of the mold to prevent the stem from becoming a permanent part of the mold.

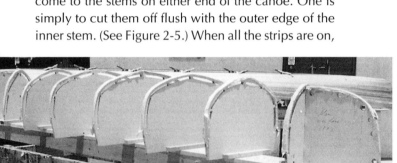

Figure 2-3: The building board, with molds erected and their edges taped to prevent the planking strips from becoming glued to the setup. The board is mounted at a convenient height on a special frame fitted with casters to make it portable. The entire rig can be easily moved outdoors when it is time to sand the hull.

Figure 2-4: The first strip on each side of the hull in place. Note that one strip has been beveled on the end and the other strip, unbeveled, runs right past it. When the hull is completely planked, the ends are belt sanded fair and the gap between the inner stem and the point where the strips make contact is filled with epoxy.

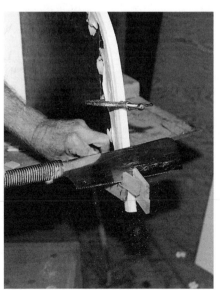

Figure 2-5a and Figure 2-5b: Another way to handle the strips at the stem is to simply cut off the ends flush with the face of the inner stem. This method, however, will require a wide outer stem.

you can use a belt sander to make a fair curve along the inner stem face, and laminate an outer stem to cover the ends of the strips. The outer stem has to be pretty wide to do this, however, and creates a blunt end on your boat.

The other way is the method I use on all my boats now. It is to let the strip on one side run by the stems on both ends of the boat. I line up my handsaw with the bevel of the stem and the first mold, and cut the end of the strip to that same bevel. The strip on the other side is allowed to run by this strip, glued to the inner stem and the opposing strip, and then cut off square. (See Figure 2-4.) Switch the side that is allowed to run by with each pair of strips.

At the stems, when all the strips are on, a belt sander can be used to fair the curve, but now we have an outer stem that is only ³⁄₈ inch wide, which I feel looks a lot neater. The gap between the inner stem and the point where the strips make contact will be filled with epoxy when we work on the inside of the boat.

Strip planking goes quickly. All this so far took me almost as long to write as it does to do. On the first day of my annual class at WoodenBoat School, where I teach a course on building the Wee Lassie, with the building board already made and laid out, the students are able to make their molds, bevel the inner stems, and start stripping the boat by noon of the first day.

But don't rush. Take your time. Watch the shape of the boat evolve as you go along. Any time I build a canoe of a different design or a new rowing shell, I find it fascinating to see the change as the boat comes off the drawing board and becomes a living creation, rather than a collection of lines on a piece of paper.

Stripping the Hull

Glue is applied to the cove side of each succeeding strip. The easiest way to do this is to rout a groove in a 2 by 4 to hold the strip as carpenter's glue is spread on it. (See Figure 2-6.) You can apply glue directly from the squeeze container the glue comes in, or you might find it easier to transfer the glue to a small syringe and use that. Make sure the entire surface of the cove is covered. Do this by lightly running your finger down the strip, evening out the glue. Remove the strip from the grooved 2 by 4, lay it cove side down on the strip below it, and squeeze it in place. Before nailing it or clamping it securely, check to be sure both ends of the strip stick out far enough past the inner stems to be trimmed properly.

If you will be nailing the strips temporarily to the molds, use one nail with a block at each mold and

¹⁄₄-inch staples across the joint in the spaces between the molds. (See Figure 2-7.) One staple between the molds will usually suffice to keep the joint tight until the glue sets up. Don't use staples longer than ¹⁄₄ inch, as they will come through on the inside; when you wipe off the excess glue on the inside of the strips, the protruding staples will cut you like a razor.

Clean up all excess glue as you go along. This not only makes the hull look better while being stripped, but also will save you money in sanding discs, as well as time when you sand the hull.

If you will be clamping strips to the molds, you can use shock cord to pull the strips tightly between the molds, rather than the staples ordinarily used. Drill a ¹⁄₄-inch hole in a short block of wood, run a 36-inch piece of shock cord through the hole, and tie a knot in the end to keep it from pulling out. Clamp the block to the first strip or two, then you can just pull the cord over the strip to be pulled down, and cinch it tightly. (See Figure 2-8.)

No matter which system you use — nails or clamps — make sure the cove edge of the strip is firmly set onto the bead of the strip below and is not just riding up on one of the featheredges. You want the glue to squeeze out uniformly.

If you will be adding a feature strip as described in the previous chapter, keep in mind its placement. I usually install the feature strip as the fourth strip up from the sheer strip, but there is no hard-and-fast rule. The location is, of course, up to you, the builder. So, too, is the decision whether to use one or not. I feel that a feature strip, if only a contrasting piece of wood, adds considerable appeal to the boat. People have always decorated their tools, weapons, pots, baskets, themselves, and of course, their boats. And why not? What prettier object have people ever designed and built than the boats they paddle, row, and sail?

The Bottom Strips

As you approach the bottom of the canoe, the strips become more difficult to control. I find it very helpful to use small C-clamps and scrap-wood blocks to help hold the ends of the strips tightly to the stems. Follow up with additional clamps as you go on with the stripping. Spring clamps, which are like additional hands, can also be a big help.

I use a keel or center strip to control the rocker, or the fore-and-aft curve, of the bottom of the hull, as well as the fairness of the transition that occurs at the top of each stem mold. (See Figure 2-9.) Each boat will vary slightly at this point, but the illustrations show how this tricky area is handled. If the inner stem gets in the way, there is nothing wrong with cutting it down a little with a chisel. The keel strip is cut to fit down in between the two side strips at each end, and glued and stapled in place. From this point on, the ends of the

Figure 2-6: Running a bead of glue down the coved side of a strip. To simplify the operation, the strip is sitting in a groove routed into a 2 by 4.

Figure 2-7a and Figure 2-7b: Here, the strips are being held in place with nails driven through scrap blocks into the edges of the molds, and with staples across the seams. Note the excess glue along the seam; this should be cleaned off before it cures.

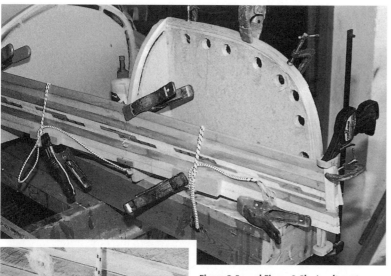

Figure 2-8a and Figure 2-8b: An alternate method is to use spring clamps to hold the strips against the molds and shock cords to hold the strips tightly together while the glue sets up. A block clamped to the sheer holds one end of the shock cord; the other end is looped over, cinched down, and held with a half hitch.

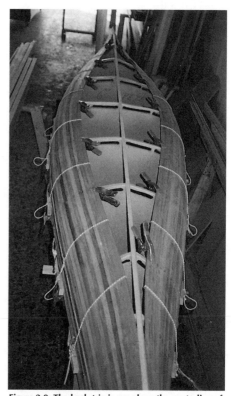

Figure 2-9: The keel strip is run along the centerline of the molds and then the ends of the planking strips on each side are fitted to it as they are laid.

side strips are cut to fit the keel strip. (See Figure 2-10.)

Cutting the strips to fit into the keel or center strip takes time and care. I use a Japanese Dozuki saw to make these cuts. The Dozuki is designed to cut on the pull stoke. The blade is extremely thin, yet it doesn't bind. Japanese saws were once difficult to obtain, but now they are carried by most of the catalog tool suppliers (see Appendix C). If one of your strips doesn't fit perfectly against the center strip, a new saw cut made with the strips in place should create a perfect joint.

When you are working with carpenter's glue and sometimes resawing joints, the fine teeth of a Dosuki saw can become clogged with glue. To prevent this, I keep the blade pretty well doused with WD-40. If you don't keep the blade clean, you will spend a lot of money on replacement blades. Cutting through staples and nails doesn't help them any, either.

The Outer Stems and Removing the Nails

While you are finishing up the bottom strips, laminate the outer stems in place. (See Figure 2-11.) I generally use cherry, ripped thin so it will bend easily, and hold the laminations in place with nails, clamps, and shock cord until the glue sets.

When the glue has had time to set on everything, you can pull all the nails and staples. I use a tack puller and a pair of nippers for this operation. (See Figure 2-12.) Be neat. If you drop staples and nails all over the floor, you will pick them up in your shoe soles and heels and deposit them on the first carpet you walk on. This can be extremely hard on bare feet at a later date.

You are now ready to plane and sand the hull in preparation for a covering of epoxy and fiberglass cloth.

Planing and Sanding the Hull

I use a sharp block plane, set very fine, to clean up the hull. The goal is to remove any globs of glue, most of the glue stains, and any high edges on the strips. I usually use the plane with a shearing motion, holding it at about a 45-degree angle to the strips. Take your time with this. Now you will begin to see how pretty your little boat will be when finished.

Be careful that you do not plane too much wood off the surface of the hull. You definitely do not want any areas to become so thin that you will be able to see through them when the boat is turned over.

A few words of caution before sanding the hull: Wood dust is definitely hazardous to your health, so you should always wear a face mask when sanding, even when you are working outside in the fresh air. No one wants to die of lung cancer. You can use an inexpensive paper mask, but I prefer the type with renewable filters. Get a mask that is comfortable, so you will wear it.

Besides using a face mask when sanding, I also have a homemade air filter in my shop that helps to control the amount of dust in the air. These are commercially obtainable now, and sources for them are listed in Appendix C. I will be having one of these air filters in any shop I ever own.

The best tool for sanding the hull is a random-orbit sander, which looks like a disc sander, but the action is different. As a result it doesn't leave the swirl marks left by a disc sander. The model I prefer is the 6-inch Porter Cable number 7336, with an adjustable speed control. I never use the sanding pad that comes with the machine, as it is too stiff for the job at hand. Rather, I use a contour pad made by Porter Cable for the sander; this works just fine.

Sanding is done to eliminate any glue stains and, of course, to smooth down any ridges left by the block plane. Start sanding with a 36-or 40-grit disc. Keep the pad moving, and keep it flat on the wood. Don't dig in with the edges of the pad. I usually keep the adjustable speed control set at 5, rather than at top speed. This makes the sander easier to control.

Before I switch to a disc with a finer grit I usually spend an hour or two board-sanding the boat. I made my own board, and you can, too. Use a 1-inch board, approximately 4 inches wide by 36 inches long; glue coarse-grit sandpaper on one face and a handle on the other. With this tool, worked in long, sweeping motions, you can remove any high spots and produce a nicely fair hull. (See Figure 2-13.)

This is a good time to fill any nail holes with toothpicks. I use the type that are square in section in the center and round at the ends. Broken in half, they work just great. Push them into the little holes, tap them lightly into place with a hammer, and break them off with the side of your hand. (See Figure 2-14.) I don't bother with the staple holes, as they are so small they will become filled with epoxy when we give the hull a sealer coat.

Now switch to an 80-grit disc on the random-orbit sander and resand the hull carefully. This will take out any swirl marks left by the coarser disc and the sanding board and, with luck, all the remaining glue stains.

If there are any bad spots on the hull — dings,

gaps between strips, etc. — now is a good time to fill them. You can use a mixture of sanding dust and Rock Hard wood putty powder, mixed into a little catalyzed epoxy resin. Or if you are using West System epoxy, you can use a mix of their filleting blend and lightweight filler. The best material I have found for any patching operation, however, is Wood Flour, sold by System Three. If you mix your own filler, try to create a neutral color — not too light, not too dark. Plain wood dust or sawdust is unsatisfactory; they are coarse, and will turn too dark when sealed with epoxy.

Whatever filler you use, always mix epoxy for two minutes before adding the filler. Otherwise, the epoxy might not cure properly and you could have a mess. (I have much, much more to say about handling epoxy in the next chapter.)

Rather than making a mess with your fingers or a putty knife, apply the filler with a small syringe, available from your epoxy supplier. This will give you more control.

Allow the filler to set up overnight, then sand away any stain left by the epoxy mixture outside the fill area. At the same time, make sure there are no glue stains remaining on the hull, as they will show through the finish if they are not removed completely. A stain cannot be removed after the sealer coat is applied, so this is your last chance.

I really enjoy running my hands over the hull at this stage. The wood is soft and warm to the touch. Finished, yet not protected from the elements. Lovely, but still fragile. We are about to change the fragile part.

Figure 2-10: The ends of the planking strips must be carefully fitted against the sides of the keel strip. A Japanese Dozuki, which cuts on the pull stroke, is ideal for this.

Figure 2-11: The outer stem is laminated over the inner stem and the faired-off ends of the strip planking. When the glue has cured it will be faired to shape.

Figure 2-12: Using a tack puller to remove all the fastenings.

Figure 2-14 Nail holes are plugged with toothpicks.

Figure 2-13: Using a sanding board to fair the outside surface of the hull. Follow this with an 80-grit disc in a random-orbit sander.

On the wall of my shop I have several poster-sized photographs of some of my favorite canoeing spots. They serve as a reminder of great places I have been, and as an introduction to my students of the different world they are entering now that they are building their own canoes.

Most of my favorite places are not the popular ones. You won't find them described in the canoe magazines. Some are out of the way and difficult to find without good directions; others are close to population centers, but they are little known or used. They exist in every region I have been in our beautiful country. No matter where you live, if you look, you will find places like them. I receive letters from Wee Lassie owners all over the world, from Scotland to South Africa, describing some of the really neat places they paddle. Interesting water is everywhere.

One way I judge a particular area is by the degree of enchantment I feel as I paddle. This is difficult to quantify and extremely difficult to describe, but wonderful to experience. To me, to be in what I consider the best of the best paddling territory is to gain spiritual renewal.

When I was a little boy, some people used to talk about being in a State of Grace. I never understood what they were talking about. I feel as if I do now. That feeling comes on the Ichetucknee River.

Dale Andrews, one of my students who over the years has become a real friend, describes the Ichetucknee, on a scale of one to ten, as a twenty. I couldn't agree more.

The Ichetucknee, like most of Florida's small spring-fed rivers, is only four or five miles long. It is located between Tallahassee and Gainesville, about halfway down the Florida peninsula. I usually start my trip on the river at the point considered by most canoeists as the take out. I paddle upstream to the springs and then drift back down with the current. That makes the trip last longer and is one of the big advantages of a small, double-paddle canoe. You can paddle upstream against a current with very little effort and avoid having to ferry vehicles and your canoe from one end of a stream to the other.

Why do I like the Ichetucknee so much? That's

simple to answer. The river is pristine. The water is crystal clear. The first time I visited the spring at the entrance to the park by canoe, I thought the water was covered with duckweed or filled with green algae. Then, with a shock, I realized I was looking at the sparkling green of water plants on the bottom of the river, 20 feet below the surface.

The last time I was on the Ichetucknee, with the exception of a single beer can, it was spotless. No Styrofoam cartons, no lunch wrappers, no trash of any kind. The people who run the park stop the trash problem before it becomes a problem: they don't allow you to take anything with you in your canoe. Their theory is that if you don't have the makings of trash with you, you can't leave trash in or on the river. (Maybe we ought to apply this system on a wider scale; modify the education system in this country instead of building more jails.) Thanks to the topnotch work of the park crew, the Ichetucknee's water is crystal clear for its entire length.

This is a stream to savor. It twists and turns its way through heavily wooded areas and open, marshy glades, with surprises around every bend. I almost always see deer along the banks. The bird life is typical of Florida depending on the season. But it is the otters that always fascinate me. To watch a mother otter guarding her pups while they forage through the water plants for crawfish and frogs is to me a great experience.

I have never seen an alligator on this stretch of the Ichetucknee. You might find them outside the park boundaries on the way to the Santa Fe River, but not this close to the springs. That's probably why the otters flourish.

In the summertime the Ichetucknee is mainly given over to people floating downstream in inner tubes. Years ago college kids from Gainesville would load up their inner tubes with cases of beer and party heavily as they floated down the river. They had great fun, but they were ruining the habitat. Now the tubers still get to enjoy the scenery and, thanks to the no-cargo rule, the stream stays pristine for the next person to enjoy.

I prefer to paddle the Ichetucknee on weekdays in the late fall, winter, and early spring. (One of the few real benefits of getting older and being semi-retired is being able to paddle during the week, when the young people are in school and their parents are working.) Usually I go early in the morning, sometimes on days that most people would consider to be too cold. I share the stream with the otters and no one else. That may sound selfish, but it's a great experience.

The Ichetucknee is easy to get to. On Route 75 between Gainesville and Lake City, turn onto Route 27 and head west toward Tallahassee. When you reach the park, you'll see a big building and a very large parking lot for the hordes of tubers who use this stream in the summer. Go past the parking lot, where the tubers board trams for the trip up to the springs. About a half mile farther there is another turnoff, not as well marked, just before a bridge that crosses the stream. Pull in there and park. It is a very short carry to the stream. The parking lot has always been safe, which is important to me as I usually have a van full of camping equipment and paddling gear, to say nothing of tools if I am on my way somewhere else to teach a class on canoe building.

If you go past this parking lot, take the next right turn, and then take the next right again; you will arrive at the main entrance to the park where the springs are located. You can launch your canoe there if you only want to go downstream.

BACK TO WORK

CHAPTER THREE

Epoxy Work

Now is the time to begin serious work with epoxy resin and fiberglass. I have found that most boatbuilders worry about this part of the project if they have had no prior experience with it. They have gone to great lengths to get this far, and they worry about spoiling their beautiful hull.

There is no need to worry. Epoxy work is not difficult if you follow fairly simple rules. But they are rules.

Remember that you seek a clear finish that will let the natural beauty of the wood show through. Some of the hardeners sold for use with epoxy are excellent for a clear finish, and some are not. Be careful about the advice you receive from people who use epoxies for purposes other than clear coating. I received too much very bad advice when I started building my first canoes and therefore had to learn the hard way about what did and did not work.

Some hardeners absorb moisture from the air and release it later to create cloudy areas in the finish. There is no way to clear up these areas without sanding the epoxy coating back down, possibly to bare wood. This is not fun.

Rules to Remember

There are a few simple rules in using epoxy, and I will cover them here.

Protect your eyes. When stirring or doing anything with epoxy, do not splash it around or flip it off your squeegee, as it can get into your eyes or the eyes of someone nearby. Epoxy can cause permanent damage to your vision. Washing it out won't help much,

23

but do it anyway, with clean water. Then get to a doctor immediately.

Wear gloves whenever you are using epoxy. I know they can be hot and make your hands sweat. Let them sweat. Epoxy can be absorbed through the skin, and then it can reside permanently in various organs of the body. Be wary of cheap throw-away gloves; I prefer the ones recommended by my epoxy supplier. These are latex gloves, which are about 30 percent more resistant to chemical penetration and are far superior to vinyl.

To protect your arms, Gougeon Brothers, the company that supplies my epoxy, offers throw-away sleeves you can slip over your forearms. They help keep your arms epoxy free when you are working with fiberglass cloth up in the bow and stern, inside the boat. These disposable sleeves are cooler than a long-sleeved shirt and certainly are cheaper in the long run, unless you have a lot of old workshirts lying around.

Don't treat epoxy like paint. Most people wait until they are through painting, and then clean their brushes and hands with mineral spirits or paint thinner. Don't plan to do that with epoxy. Using acetone or other thinners only makes it easier for the epoxy to penetrate your skin. Therefore, work clean. Long sleeves or protective clothing are fine in cooler climates but may be too much for you to stand in very hot weather. In the latter case, dress for the weather and be really careful not to get any epoxy on your skin.

Vapors from the epoxy sold for amateur use do not smell bad, but they are still toxic. Make sure you have good ventilation, and/or wear a face mask with a charcoal filter. My shop has excellent cross ventilation. As of this date I have had no health problems from epoxy that I am aware of, even though I have been using the resin on a regular basis for the last decade and a half.

Measure epoxy carefully. It is smart to buy and use the simple measuring pumps that most epoxy manufacturers have available. Don't ever think that by adding a little more hardener you will speed up the curing process. This does not work with epoxy. All it does is upset the chemistry and results in a weak mix at best, and a sticky mess at worst.

When installing measuring pumps in a can of epoxy or hardener, it pays to trim the ends of the extender tubes square across with a razor blade. The tubes have been cut on a bevel in the factory and tend to split during use, giving improper resin-hardener ratios.

When you combine the components — the epoxy and the hardener — stir the mixture vigorously for at least two minutes. You don't want to whip the epoxy into a froth, but you do want to mix the hardener thoroughly into the epoxy. If you fail to stir the epoxy and hardener properly, you can end up with epoxy that stays sticky forever, a mess that is extremely difficult to remove without spoiling the boat. To make sure I am thorough, I use a simple egg timer given to me by one of my students.

I use and recommend Gougeon Brothers West System epoxy and supplies because they are consistent. Gougeon's products are higher priced than those of most of their competitors, but I feel that consistent high quality is more important than price. I believe it is foolish to risk ruining a lot of hard work just to save a few dollars in material costs. I am lucky to have a reliable, local supplier of Gougeon products; anything that I order before nine o'clock in the morning is delivered to my shop before noon of the same day. This combination of dependability and service makes this product line worth every penny to me.

Gougeon Brothers manufactures several different hardeners. If you want a clear finish on your canoe, use the 207 Special Coating Hardener. Their other hardeners become cloudy under certain conditions. When you are using epoxy as glue only, cloudiness doesn't matter, but it does when you are using it to clear-coat a cedar-strip canoe.

The main point to be sure about is that the epoxy you use, regardless of the brand, has been designed to produce a clear finish — or, I should say, the hardener, because I believe the epoxy itself is pretty much standard.

Even though polyester resin is cheaper, do not use it. Polyester does not bond properly to wood and can quickly delaminate, spoiling your canoe.

Tools and Materials Required

To cover a Wee Lassie canoe, you will need 10 yards of 4-ounce fiberglass cloth and — assuming you are using Gougeon Brothers products — a gallon of epoxy and a third of a gallon of 207 hardener. If you are using another brand of epoxy that has a different mixing ratio, order enough to total 1 1/3 gallons. All directions given from here on, however, will be for Gougeon products, because I am familiar with them.

You will also need several clean containers, gloves, several spreaders, a roller, roller covers, 3-inch foam brushes, a pair of scissors, and single-edge razor blades. You can buy the containers from your supplier, but I use cans from home. Clean cat-food cans are great, as are 15-ounce food cans; their use saves money and recycles material that would otherwise to go the dump.

Don't use cheap roller covers from a paint store for epoxy work. They will come apart and make a mess. Use black-foam roller covers, or much better, the yellow covers that Gougeon supplies. I cut these in half and use them with the type of short roller handle that painters use for trim. Most paint stores carry these.

I make no attempt to clean the rollers or foam brushes. It would cost more for solvents than it would be worth, and almost all solvents are dangerous to your health. I am so leery of solvents that I don't even like to have them in my shop.

Sealing the Surface

Before mixing any epoxy check the hull one more time for glue stains before you seal it and lock in the coloration forever. (See Figure 3-1.) The only tool you will need for the sealing operation is a plastic spreader. To make it easier to hold in use, sand the center of the spreader lightly.

Before touching either the resin or the hardener, put your gloves on!

Pump ten strokes of hardener and ten of epoxy into a clean can or container, and stir vigorously for at least two minutes. When pumping the components, get in the habit of pumping one stroke of hardener and then one of epoxy. Then, even if you get distracted and lose count, you will at least still have the proper proportions, and that is the most important thing. I learned this trick from Larry Page, a good friend, while I was teaching him how to build his canoe. I learn a lot from my students.

One of the main points I try to teach my students is to get the epoxy out of the can and onto the boat as quickly as possible. Catalyzed epoxy that is confined in a container heats up quickly and becomes unusable. Once it has been spread out in a thin coat over the entire boat, you will have plenty of time to work with it. I usually start spreading the resin in the middle of the canoe, but stay on one side of the centerline until I finish covering that side of the boat completely.

You want the sealer coat to sink into the wood. I go around the hull several times with the spreader to move any excess epoxy onto areas where the wood is sucking it in. You want to cover the territory completely without creating runs and drips, which will have to be sanded off.

After allowing the epoxy a couple of minutes to soak in, lightly clean off any excess with the spreader.

Use a 3-inch foam brush or a clump of paper towels to wipe out any ridges left by the spreader.

Allow this coat to dry overnight. In the morning you can sand it lightly in preparation for the fiberglass cloth. For this I use an 80-grit disc in a random-orbit sander. Don't sand down to the wood; you just want to roughen the epoxy.

Fiberglassing the Outside of the Hull

When you think you have sanded enough, vacuum off any dust and roll out the fiberglass cloth over the boat. Before you cut the cloth, make sure the piece is long enough to cover both ends. Smooth out any wrinkles by hand. (See Figure 3-2.) You can trim off most of the excess cloth, but don't cut too closely at

Figure 3-1: The faired and sanded hull, ready for an epoxy sealer coat and a layer of fiberglass cloth.

Figure 3-2: Smoothing-on the fiberglass cloth.

this stage. Leave at least an inch or so of extra cloth all the way around.

When applying epoxy to dry fiberglass cloth, I always use a new, unused spreader. The edge on an old one could be rough and could tend to pull at the cloth, possibly spreading the weave and causing difficulty in achieving a clear finish. For the same reason I always use fresh gloves when applying the saturation coat to fiberglass cloth.

The amount of epoxy required to saturate the cloth is twice the amount used to seal the wood. When you spread the epoxy, it is important at first to keep all the epoxy on one side of the hull. I try to wet out the cloth on one side and get that side completely under control before I do anything on the other side of the boat. If you are sloppy and allow epoxy to run all over both sides at once, the operation can get totally out of hand.

Mix up ten squirts of epoxy and hardener, which should be enough to cover one side of the Wee Lassie. I start in the middle of one side and spread the epoxy over the 'glass with a spreader, working outward toward both ends. (See Figures 3-3 and 3-4.) As before, you want to get the epoxy out of the can quickly and onto the boat. At the same time, you want to saturate the cloth completely as you go. Don't leave any areas unsaturated behind you; these can be difficult to work with later without causing wrinkles. The fiberglass cloth seems to disappear as it is saturated, and the wood shows through again.

Pay attention to what you are doing, and don't allow yourself to be distracted. If the telephone rings, don't answer it. I don't believe an audience helps at this stage of the game, either. Don't panic, and don't get in a rush. Don't try to micro-finish one end of the hull while ignoring the other end of the boat.

When the fiberglass cloth on the first side of the boat is completely saturated, you can use up any excess resin on the center of the other side before mixing up another ten-pump batch of epoxy to finish the job.

When both sides of the boat are completely wetout, go around the entire boat gently with the spreader to even out the epoxy coverage. You don't want runny areas where the epoxy is too thick, but on the other hand you should not have any cloudy areas where the epoxy is too thin. The ideal is to have the cloth completely wetout, with the texture of the cloth just barely apparent.

At this stage of the job, I use my gloved hands to gently work out any wrinkles in the cloth. Start in the middle of the boat and work on each side toward the

ends of the boat, as well as toward the sheer. The cloth will slide a little over the wood ahead of your hands.

When all the wrinkles have been worked out and there are no apparent runs in the epoxy, it is time to trim the cloth at the stems. Do not attempt to wrap the cloth around the stems, as it will create a mess. I use a single-edge razorblade to make a neat cut about ¼-inch back from the outer edges of the stems and then pull off the excess.

To cover the stems, cut some strips from scrap fiberglass cloth on the bias — i.e., at an angle of 45 degrees to the weave. These strips should be about 3 inches wide by about 12 inches long. Place them on wax paper and wet them out with epoxy, then cover both stems with at least two layers and smooth out any air bubbles. The bias-cut strips will wrap around the curved areas of the stems without any problems, while regular fiberglass tape, not cut on the bias, will not.

Relax now and admire your work while you wait for the resin to become tacky.

Filling the Weave

The next coat of epoxy is applied to fill the weave of the cloth. The saturation coat doesn't have to be completely cured for this, only tacky. I wait until my finger sticks a little to the epoxy but none of it comes away. I then mix up another batch of epoxy; the same amount used for the sealer coat will do.

The filler coat should be applied with a roller, as you don't want to disturb the still-soft saturation coat and the fiberglass cloth. When you have rolled a nice even coat over the entire boat, use a foam brush to take out any bubbles left by the roller.

At this time you can trim the cloth at the sheerline with a razor blade, being careful not to disturb the cloth in any way. (See Figure 3-5.) Then leave the boat alone, and let the epoxy harden.

The Final Coats

The following day, sand the boat lightly with an 80-grit disc in a random-orbit sander. All you want to do is roughen the epoxy. Don't sand deeply, and by all means don't sand deep enough to touch or cut into the cloth.

After vacuuming off any dust, apply two more coats of epoxy with a roller, brushing out the bubbles with a foam brush and waiting between coats for the surface to become tacky.

Your boat should be looking great by now. Let the

last coat of epoxy cure overnight at least, and then you can release the hull from the molds.

Cleaning Up and Sealing the Inside

If you were careful to tape the edges of the molds before stripping, the hull should release from the molds without any difficulty. I usually tap the molds loose, and then gently pry up each end of the hull.

The hull should weigh about ten or so pounds at this stage, so one person can handle it easily. It will also be a little limber, as there is fiberglass cloth on only one side, but we will soon fix that. Set the hull right-side up in slings for support, and go to work on the interior. (See Figure 3-6.)

I clean off most of the odds and ends of masking tape and globules of glue left on the inside of the canoe with a round-edge scraper. If you have one, use a wooden, round-bottom plane to take off any high plank edges before you start sanding. This type of plane is difficult to find and usually has to be homemade. The only ones I know of that are commercially manufactured are offered by Japan Woodworker (see Appendix C); the price is about $60.

Use a random-orbit sander with a 36-grit disc to clean out the inside. (See Figure 3-7.) Take your time, and use a dust mask. The goal here is to eliminate any high edges on the strips that would create a void between the fiberglass cloth and the wood, and to remove any

Figure 3-3: Working the resin into the fiberglass cloth with a plastic spreader. Get the resin out of the can quickly and onto the boat. Work on one side of the boat at a time, from the middle toward the ends.

Figure 3-4: Working along toward the stem. After the cloth has been completely wetout, I will be going back over the areas with puddled and ridged resin and smoothing them out with the spreader.

Figure 3-5: The outside of the hull, including the stems, has been coated with epoxy and the excess cloth at the sheer is ready to be trimmed off. The resin has caused the fiberglass cloth to turn transparent, allowing the beauty of the wood to show through.

Figure 3-6: The hull has been removed from the molds, and the inside is ready to be scraped and sanded. The stands are made from 2 by 4s; the slings are scrap carpeting fastened to the uprights with blocks.

Figure 3-7: Sanding the inside of the hull with a random-orbit sander prior to the sealer coat.

glue stains that will show through the epoxy.

When the hull has been sanded and vacuumed dust-free, seal the inside with epoxy. Here again, you should let the resin soak into the wood but not lie in puddles along the bottom. Puddles of epoxy don't add strength, only weight.

Fiberglassing the Inside

When you are ready to 'glass the inside of the boat, roll out the cloth and cut it a little shorter than the length of the boat. Full-length cloth tends to bunch up and make a horrible mess in the difficult-to-reach areas behind the stems. It is far easier to keep the cloth back a little from the inner stems and use bias strips to cover these areas after the main fiberglass is well epoxied in place.

Allow the cloth to drape down into the hull and carefully smooth out as many wrinkles as possible. (See Figure 3-8.)

Mix up about ten pumps of epoxy and hardener, but this time pour it all out on the centerline of the boat. Work the epoxy up the sides to the sheer with a spreader, and work from the center toward the ends of the boat, completely saturating the cloth as you go. (See Figure 3-9.) Move the excess epoxy ahead of you. You do not want the 'glass to float on a thick layer of epoxy, which adds weight but not strength. When you run out of epoxy, mix up another batch and continue to saturate the cloth into both ends. Smooth any wrinkles out with your gloved hands, as you did on the exterior of the boat. (See Figures 3-10 and 3-11.) Use a foam brush or a wad of paper towels to mop up any areas where epoxy is pooling in the bottom of the boat, or making runs down the sides.

A long bubble will usually try to form on the bottom of the canoe at the end of each inner stem. If it does, slice the bubble with a single-edge razorblade, thus enabling the 'glass to lie flat against the wood. After the fiberglass and epoxy have had some time to set up, we can drop back and take care of the ends of the boat.

Cut strips from scrap fiberglass cloth on the bias, wet them out on wax paper, and fold them into the bow and stern of the canoe. Epoxy will tend to pool at the ends of each inner stem, so soak up any excess with a paper towel. Cleaning up as you go saves a lot of sanding later, and this is a hard-to-reach spot.

I usually don't double-coat the inside of the boat as I do the outside, as I think it might lead to a build-up of excess epoxy in the bottom of the boat. This epoxy would have no place else to go, whereas on the outside of the boat, if you apply too much epoxy, at least it will drip off onto the floor.

The next day, after the epoxy has set up, sand the surface lightly and apply another coat. I use a spreader to lay this coat on, then a roller to even out the epoxy, followed by a foam brush to wipe out any bubbles left by the roller. Then I wait until after the rails and decks are on before applying a final epoxy coat on the interior.

Odds and Ends

Some builders skip the sealing coat and wet out the wood and the cloth at the same time. This works if you are careful. If you aren't careful, the wood will tend to suck the epoxy out of the cloth, creating resin-starved areas. I believe that sealing the wood first, lightly sanding, and then applying the fiberglass works the best.

Never try to spread fiberglass cloth over a surface that has already been coated and is still wet or tacky. This could make getting out any wrinkles impossible and could cause major difficulties.

Cold temperatures are seldom a problem here in Florida, where my shop is located. We do get 32-degree temperatures for short periods in the winter. The general rule of thumb I follow is not to fiberglass a boat when I am wearing more than one sweatshirt. On occasion I have to use a small electric heat gun to warm up the epoxy and hardener before use, but this is mainly to make sure the pump works properly so the epoxy proportions are correct. I also tend to stir the resin and the hardener a little longer in cool weather. The advantage of cooler temperatures is that they slow down the curing time of the epoxy, so I have more time to work with it; I also have to wait longer between coats.

Do not ever work with epoxy in direct sunshine; you will get a million bubbles.

I find 70 to 80 degrees F to be the perfect temperature range for epoxy work. When the temperature gets up around 90 and over, I don't have much time to mess around and must pay close attention to what I am doing. I have never been caught by the 207 hardener kicking off too soon, even on much larger boats than the Wee Lassie, but that is because I have everything well organized before I starting catalyzing epoxy.

To sum up, the secrets of successfully working with epoxy are simple:

Measure precisely.

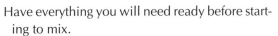

Have everything you will need ready before starting to mix.

Mix thoroughly for at least two minutes.

Get the resin out of the mixing container as quickly as possible.

Limit the area you are covering to an area you
can handle.

Eliminate distractions.

Pay attention to the temperature in the area you
are working in. If cold is a problem, use a safe
heater or wait until warmer weather.

Clean up any drips or runs as you go along, as
they are difficult to sand out later.

For safety's sake:
    Protect your eyes.
    Wear gloves.
    Work clean.

Figure 3-8: Fiberglass
cloth is draped into
the interior and held
with spring clamps to
prevent it from shift-
ing. Here, it has been
cut a trifle long, and
the bunching behind
the inner stem is
obvious.

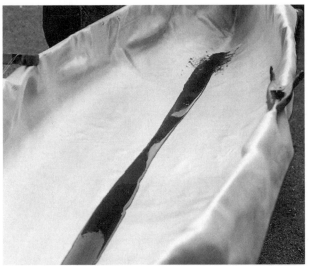
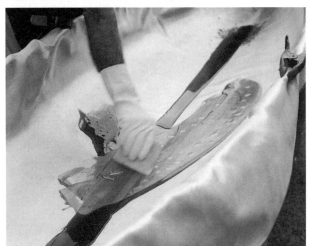

Figure 3-9a and Figure 3-9b: The epoxy is poured all along the center of the keel and then spread up the sides and toward the ends.

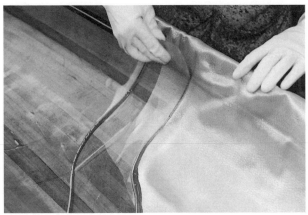

Figure 3-10: Use one hand to keep the cloth from puckering while spreading the epoxy with the other. Stay calm and be methodical.

Figure 3-11: As on the outside of the hull, go back over the inside with the
spreader to smooth out any puddles and ridges once the fiberglass has
been thoroughly saturated.

Central Florida has several other really nice spring-fed streams to paddle besides the lovely Ichetucknee River. Three that I like are in the Ocala area, just off Route 75. Turn off onto Route 40, and drive through Ocala to Silver Springs. On the far side of Silver Springs, just before the massive bridge over the Oklawaha River, there is a public park, which is safe as far as I know, and a spot to put-in.

The first section of your voyage is down a short, dirty canal, but quickly you emerge into a bright green jungle. I'm talking about being inside an emerald. The trees overhead are bright green, and the water plants below the surface are bright green. You are floating in-between.

I am talking about Paradise. A flawed paradise, but still a great place to paddle. At the end of this section you can paddle upstream against the current on the Silver River run, or go with the current into the Oklawaha River.

The Oklawaha is a great river to paddle as it is fairly narrow and, for the most part, tree covered. (During the summer in Florida, you really want that tree cover for shade from the hot sun.) There is very little development on the Oklawaha, as most of the river is inside a state forest. On the weekends, however, there are a lot of fisherman in powerboats. For one-way canoeists, there is an outfitter upstream

at Fort McCoy who furnishes transportation and a safe place to park for a reasonable fee.

The Oklawaha almost became a part of the Florida Barge Canal, and parts of it have been turned into shallow lakes, but this section is still wild. Small steamboats used to ply this stream from St. Augustine and Jacksonville. The travelers had great sport shooting at the thousands of birds and hundreds of alligators that sunned on the banks.

Some of the birds and alligators remain. I have often seen one of my favorite raptors, the swallow-tailed kite, on this river. White, with its wings tipped in black, and a very definite swallowtail, this is a beautiful bird to watch soar over a river.

Earlier on, if you were to turn upstream, rather than downstream on the Oklawaha, you can paddle about four miles on a crystal-clear stream, through a

tropical jungle of cypress trees. You should see deer, otter, and much bird life. Monkeys, believe it or not, are another attraction. They were brought in years ago for the early Tarzan movies, which were filmed on the river. They went wild, and now live freely in the trees alongside the river and are great fun to watch. This is a lovely paddle, spoiled only by the presence of motorboats.

Motorboats can no longer go full speed along this stretch, as they used to, but are required to maintain no-wake speeds at all times. This is a big improvement to safety, but the boats' smell lingers on; the slower they go, the smellier their exhaust. The noise can sometimes be annoying, too, as it disrupts the peace and quiet that I seek and cherish when I paddle.

Soon you will come into a large area of springs, but you must stay in your boat, as all the land surrounding the springs is owned by a tourist attraction. I try to paddle as early in the morning as possible while the water is still crystal clear, and before the motorboats become active. I imagine the weekend traffic is heavy.

Back in your car, if you cross the bridge over the Oklawaha River outside Silver Springs and continue on Route 40, you will come to Juniper

Springs State Park, where there is a great little stream. The trip starts right at the spring, through a very narrow and twisting waterway, and ends in a marshy area, where you can be picked up and taken back to your car at the park. There are a couple of rather large alligators in the marshy area, and they aren't afraid of people.

Treat all alligators with respect. Don't mess with them, and they won't mess with you. If your experience with alligators is limited to trips to the zoo, you have no idea how fast they can move, either in or out of the water. As their favorite food is any small four-legged animal, do not ever take a dog paddling with you in Florida, or anywhere else that alligators call home.

Another excellent place to paddle in this area is just a little south of Juniper Run at Alexander Springs State Park. Here again, you put in at the spring and paddle downstream. You can make arrangements to be picked up farther downstream.

These are only a few of the fine places in Florida, which is literally filled with lakes and rivers to explore. It is a shame that most of the people who visit the state flock to the expensive attractions, such as Disney World, when there is a totally fascinating world — real, as well as free — all around them.

BACK TO WORK

CHAPTER FOUR

Finishing off the Interior

The Wee Lassie is fitted with two rails at the gunwale — an inner and an outer rail — and for these I like to use cherry or mahogany. A softer wood such as spruce might be lighter, but it would be more likely to dent.

If you wish to save weight, you could use only a single rail, either interior or exterior. You could also save weight by fitting two short thwarts near the bow and the stern, and eliminate the decks. You could eliminate even more weight by doing away with the center thwart and using a pre-built canoe seat with backrest included. I don't recommend any of the above, because they sacrifice a lot of strength.

I no longer make a fetish of trying to see how light I can make my Wee Lassie canoes. As long as I can keep the weight under 30 pounds, I feel comfortable in adding strength and good looks to the little craft.

The inner and outer rails can be fitted directly to the top of the sheer strip, but I prefer to use spreader blocks behind the inner rail. This gives the boat a traditional look, plus it allows water, sand, and mud to drain out easily when the boat is hosed down after a day's outing. In addition, the spaces between the blocks allow you to tie gear to the inner rail so it will be out of your way but within easy reach while paddling. For example, I always put my camera in a Ziploc bag and tie it to the rail; the camera is protected from spray or rain, yet it is easy to reach.

Making the Inner Rails

To fit your rails the way I do, you must rip the rail material into five ³⁄₈-inch by ³⁄₄-inch strips, then use a round-over bit in a router or a hand plane to shape the bottom edge of two of these strips. These will become the outside rails.

Two of the remaining strips will be used for the inner rails, one for each side of the boat. The last strip is used for the blocks; cut it into 3-inch-long sections.

The two inner rails are made at the same time and clamped together until the glue cures; in other words, you will be creating a sandwich consisting of, in this order, the first inner rail, the blocks for it, the blocks for the second inner rail, and then the second inner rail itself. (See Figure 4-1.) The spacing between the blocks should be 4 inches.

Mix two squirts each of epoxy resin and hardener, and thicken it with colloidal silica until it has the consistency of soft peanut butter, then spread it on one face of each of the inner rails. Set these strips on edge on a flat surface, with the epoxied side facing in. Lay two blocks between the strips and clamp them in place, making sure there is no epoxy where the blocks make contact with each other; otherwise, you will have difficulty later when separating the two rail assemblies. Lay in the rest of the blocks, two at a time, right down the two rails, maintaining the 4-inch spacing and clamping as you go.

Allow the glue to cure overnight, then in the morning, before you separate the two rails, belt sand or hand sand off any excess epoxy and use a round-over bit in your router or a hand plane to trim the rails and blocks, top and bottom. Doing this work on the bench is easier than doing it once the rails are installed on the boat; in fact, it is impossible to rout the underside of the rails once they are installed.

When the inner rails are cleaned up and rounded over on both sides, separate the two rails and install them in your boat.

Installing the Rails

Sand the top two strips of the hull, both inside and outside. Mix up about three pumps each of epoxy resin and hardener, and thicken it as above with colloidal silica. Dab the epoxy on the inner face of each block on the inner rails, and spread any excess on the top inside strip of the boat. Clamp the rail in place, with a clamp at each block, starting in the center and working toward the ends. (See Figure 4-2.) You can, if you are in a hurry or don't have enough clamps, fasten the blocks with $3/4$-inch flathead screws driven from outside the hull. The screw heads will be covered by the outer rail, which can be screwed in place, or, if you have enough clamps, just epoxied. To eliminate using any screws, you can clamp

the inner rails and allow them to set overnight, and the next day epoxy the outer rails in place and clamp them.

The Deck Framing

Now epoxy in place the deck beams, the cross members that will support the deck. These can be spruce or cherry, $3/8$ inch by $3/4$ inch, and should be set about 14 inches back from the ends of the boat and cut to fit inside the inner rails. (See Figure 4-3.)

The beams for the curved after ends of the decks are laminated from thin pieces of cherry or another bendable wood. Cut these thin enough to bend easily, and about 32 inches long. Spread glue on three or four of these; after bending them in place as a unit, glue and clamp them to the inner rails and the crosspiece.

After the glue has set up overnight, sand the deck framing fair. Blend the curved lamination into the side rails and fair the tops of the framing so there will be no gaps between the deck and the outer rail. (This is why only the bottom edges of the outer rails, not the tops, are rounded over before installation.)

Now is the best time to make provision for bow and stern lines, or painters. Do this by drilling a $5/8$-inch hole about 2 inches back of each stem, and epoxy in a short piece of $1/2$-inch bronze, stainless-steel, or PVC pipe. I prefer to use PVC pipe, sold as water pipe in most hardware stores, as it is inexpensive, easy to handle, and it works. Once the epoxy has cured, saw off the ends of the pipe flush with the outside of the hull. (See Figure 4-4.)

Bow and Stern Bulkheads

If you want watertight bulkheads in the bow and stern to enhance the flotation of the canoe if it becomes swamped, these should be made and installed now, before the deck is in the way. Use scrap plywood or Styrofoam, cut to fit the curve of the sides; over this glue leftover cedar strips to match the rest of the boat. (See Figure 4-5.)

You can use clear plastic deck plates for hatches if you want to use the air space behind the bulkheads for storing such essentials as lunch, raingear, or a dry sweatshirt. Cut the correct size hole before installing the bulkheads.

You can also cut out a square or rectangular hole in the bulkheads, and frame the opening with $3/8$-inch by $1\frac{1}{2}$-inch molding. The hatch can be held in place with turnbuttons and weatherproofed with stick-on weather-stripping tape. Such an arrangement can be more attractive than a plastic deck plate, less expensive, and just as functional.

Check the bulkheads for final fit, trim as necessary, and epoxy them in place. Use pieces of cloth saturated in epoxy on the inside of the bulkheads to do a neat job of sealing them to the inside of the hull.

Strip-Planking the Decks

The deck strips can be laid in an infinite number of patterns. Herringbone, straight fore and aft, dark versus light, simple or complex — you can do your own thing. (See Figure 4-6.)

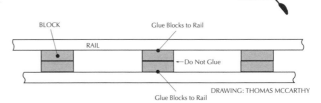

Figure 4-1: Arrangement for gluing up the rails and blocks before mounting them on the boat.

Figure 4-2: Gluing the inner and outer rails and the spreader blocks to the boat. Here, the corners of the rails and ends of the blocks have not been rounded over beforehand; they will be finished after the glue has cured.

Figure 4-3: The completed deck framing, ready for the deck planking.

Figure 4-4: Hole for bow line fitted with a section of PVC pipe. The ends of the pipe will be ground flush to the surface of the planking.

Figure 4-6: As with the hull feature strip, the careful selection of dark and light woods for planking the deck can add interest to your boat.

Figure 4-5: Styrofoam-backed bulkhead. After the deck has been planked and the hole in the bulkhead fitted with an access plate, the compartment will be watertight.

The strips can be stapled in place or clamped while the glue cures. I prefer to clamp the strips so there will be no marks from staples showing. Glue the strips to the rails and the deck framing; edge-glue them to each other as well.

After the glue has set up, use a cut-off bit in a router to trim the strips. If you don't have a router, use a saw and then a hand plane. Then sand the decks smooth.

If you have a router, you can use it to inlay a strip of dark or light wood around the outer edge of the deck. This is a nice touch and isn't at all hard to do. Set a rabbeting bit with a roller bearing to the depth of the deck strips and neatly cut a recess along both sides of the deck. Then glue in a contrasting strip and clamp it; when the glue has cured, sand this strip flush with the rest of the deck and with the rail below it.

After the decks have been sanded, use a router or hand plane to round off the top corners of the rails and decks. (See Figure 4-7.) Follow up with a random-orbit sander with an 80-grit disc to clean up everything and round off anything the router couldn't reach.

Now cover the decks with fiberglass cloth set in epoxy. Let the cloth drape down over the rails and the curved, laminated deck beam. When the cloth is completely wet out, trim it while still wet with a razor blade. Make the cut about halfway down on the rails and the curved deck beam, so everything will be locked together. Cutting the edge while it is wet lets the cloth blend into the rail.

Allow the epoxy to cure overnight, then sand lightly and brush on another coat of epoxy for a nice, clean job.

The Thwart

The thwart, which is a crossbeam that stiffens the boat and serves as a backrest, is made from the same wood as the rails. (See Figure 4-8.) The location depends on the version of the Wee Lassie you are building and is directly related to the position of the seat. In the 11-foot 6-inch version, it should be about 54 inches from the stern.

To determine the position of the seat in a double-paddle canoe, find the balance point of the hull and then locate the thwart about 16 inches back of this point. This puts the front of the seat slightly behind the balance point, which is the normal center of weight for a seated person.

Notch the thwart to fit under the rails and epoxy it in place. After the epoxy sets up, reinforce this joint with a long finish nail in a drilled hole through the rails and into the thwart; plug the hole with the same wood as the thwart, about the size of a match stick. When sanded, the plug becomes almost invisible. I think this is better than using a screw with a big bung to cover the head, and it is just as strong.

The Seat Stringer

A stringer running along the centerline of the boat is used to support the seat. For this, use a piece of 1-inch by 1½-inch by 20-inch cedar, epoxied to the bottom of the boat. Position the after end of the stringer directly under the thwart, so it will extend forward on the centerline. Two screws through the seat frame into the stringer will hold the seat in place.

The Seat

Nothing adds to the elegance of a canoe as much as a hand-caned seat. Such a seat does two things: it provides comfort and, more important, keeps your fanny dry.

When I first started building canoes, I covered the seat frames with the plastic strapping used to repair aluminum lawn chairs. This was functional but certainly not traditional.

Steve Poe, who bought one of my early canoes, insisted on cane, so I went to the local library for a book on the subject and taught myself how to cane seats. Steve's seat looked so good I have been hand caning all my seats since then.

You can buy factory-woven cane in sheets, rout a groove in the seat frame, and anchor the cane in the groove with a spline. This saves a lot of time, but I really don't like the appearance. In addition, the factory cane, which is natural material, doesn't seem to hold up as long or as well as the plastic cane that I prefer to use.

Plastic cane is resilient, holds up much better than natural cane, and is easier to use. The only problem with it is that it cannot hold knots; therefore, you must hold the loose ends from the underside of the frame with pegs.

At the time I was learning how to cane, the Wooden Canoe Heritage Association published an article in its magazine about natural versus plastic cane. The author suggested making two interchangeable seats — one with natural cane for shows and another with plastic cane for everyday use. As I build all my canoes for everyday use, the choice was made for me. I use plastic cane.

I will describe how to make a basic, square seat. If you want to get fancy, I suggest you take a trip to your local library for a complete book on caning.

Make the seat frame from the same wood as the rails and the thwart. For a Wee Lassie you will need two pieces measuring ³/₄ inch by 1 ¹/₂ inches by 22 inches, and two pieces measuring ³/₄ inch by 1 ¹/₂ inches by 12 inches. If you are making a seat for a tandem canoe, the crosspieces must be much longer and therefore should be heavier.

Mortise and tenon the frame together; the inside opening, which will be caned, should measure 11 inches square. The tenons, ³/₈ inch by 1 inch, ¹/₂ inch long, are cut into each end of the 12-inch pieces. The matching mortises are cut into the two longer framing pieces; drill them out and clean up the edges with a chisel. (See Figure 4-9.) Apply epoxy to the joints, clamp the frame, and allow to cure overnight.

Sand off any rough spots on the seat frame, then round over the edges with a router, hand plane, or sandpaper. Finish sand either by hand or by random-orbit sander.

The holes to take the cane are drilled on ⁷/₈-inch centers, set back about ⁵/₈ inch from the inner edge of the seat frame. If you will be using common-size cane, which is what I use, the holes should be ⁵/₁₆ inch diameter. Countersink the holes, top and bottom, to eliminate the sharp edge that could otherwise break the cane. Finish sand the frame, seal it with epoxy, and after the epoxy has cured properly, finish it with several coats of varnish. Now the seat is ready to be caned.

Whittle caning pegs from scrap wood. These should fit loosely in the holes for the cane and be about 2 inches long; they are used to hold the cane in place as it is being woven.

This seat requires 8 pieces of cane about 17 feet long. A 150-foot skein should be enough for the job. You will also need a little Vaseline for lubricating the cane when weaving begins, otherwise the cane will tend to cut the pieces that have already been stretched.

When people ask me how long it takes to cane a seat, I usually tell them the length of one baseball game, because I used to take my seats home and cane them while watching a ball game. After we acquired three cats, working at home became impossible, as cats are fascinated by the process of caning. I quickly found that it took an hour per cat longer to cane a seat, so now I do all the work over at my shop.

Clamp the seat frame, best side up, to a work surface at a convenient height. I like to cane standing up. Most of my students pull up a stool and take a load off their feet.

The first three steps are easy.

STEP 1

Cane is flat on one side and rounded on the other. When caning, keep the rounded side up at all times. The appearance of the finished seat will be spoiled if

Figure 4-7: Using a router to round off the corners of the rails.

Figure 4-8: One end of the thwart where it joins the inner rail.

Figure 4-9: The mortises for the seat frame are drilled first, then squared up with a chisel.

you get careless about this.

Begin by running cane across the seat from side to side. Anchor the end of a strip of cane with a wooden peg in the next hole over from a corner hole. (See Figure 4-10.) Stretch the cane across the seat and down the opposite hole, up through the next hole to it, across the seat and down the opposite hole, up through the next hole to it, and so forth. (See Figure 4-11.) Push the wooden pegs into the holes as you go to hold the cane taut. Concern yourself with the tightness of the cane, but don't worry too much about this, as the cane will tighten up considerably when weaving begins.

When you have stretched the cane through all the holes in the side framing, but not the corner holes, peg off both ends of the strip of cane.

Use pegs to anchor all subsequent strips of cane you use in the following steps.

STEP 2

With a new strip of cane, do the same thing as in Step 1, only this time run the cane — without weaving — from front to back. (See Figures 4-12 and 4-13.)

STEP 3

Repeat Step 1, running a strip of cane from side to side over the cane already stretched in Steps 1 and 2. (See Figure 4-14.)

STEP 4

This is the first weaving step. Run a strip of cane from front to back, weaving over the cane you laid down in Step 3 and under that of Step 1. (See Figure 4-15.)

STEP 5

Now run the first diagonal strip. This establishes the pattern, so take your time. Check your work against that of Figure 4-16 to make sure you are getting started on the right foot.

I don't begin the first diagonal in a corner, because I find that it is too difficult. Begin one hole over from a corner and weave diagonally across the seat and down its corresponding hole. Weave over the double side-to-side strands and under the double front-to-back strands. Come back up through the corner hole and weave diagonally back to the opposite corner and down that hole.

Here, we have a pattern change. Bring the cane back up the same hole it went down, leaving a loop below the corner. Now return to the opposite corner.

Do not weave over and under two squares at a time, even though it may make the work go quickly

and seem a lot easier. Though many people try this, it isn't seat caning and it results in a horrible-looking mess.

Figure 4-16 shows half the first diagonal weaving completed. Figure 4-17 shows how the other corner looks when the first diagonal has been completed with a second piece of cane.

The corners are the major stumbling block for anyone caning for the first time. Check your corner work against the illustrations as you go to make sure you are handling it correctly.

STEP 6

Here, you weave in the second diagonal, which runs at an angle to the first. Follow the same procedure as in Step 5, again getting started one hole away from a corner hole. Where you ran the cane under in Step 5, run it over in this step; where you ran it over in Step 5, run it under here. As above, use one piece of cane for half the seat and another for the other half.

Be wary when working the corners; when this

Figure 4-10: The first side-to-side run of cane. The peg temporarily anchors the end of the strip of cane.

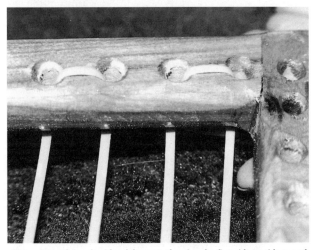

Figure 4-11: The underside of the seat, showing the first side-to-side run of cane.

Figure 4-12: The first front-to-back run of cane, which crosses over the first side-to-side run.

Figure 4-13: The underside of the seat, showing the first side-to-side and front-to-back runs.

Figure 4-14: The second side-to-side run.

Figure 4-15: The first weaving step. The cane is woven from front to back over one strip and under the next.

Figure 4-16: Half of the first diagonal strip has been woven. Note the doubling of the strands in the upper righthand and the lower lefthand corners.

Figure 4-17: The first diagonal strip has been woven, and the seat is ready for the second diagonal strip, which will run at an angle to the first.

diagonal is finished, the pattern must be the same in each of the four corners of the seat. (The complete pattern is apparent in Figure 4-18, which also shows the binder strip, described below.)

STEP 7

Now for the binder strips. Cut four pieces of cane long enough to run from corner to corner around the outside edge of the seat, with enough excess so these strips can be anchored in the corner holes. Use wooden pegs to anchor the strips temporarily.

Now, with strips of cane three times longer than the corner-to-corner binder strips, lace the binder strips in place. The lacing strip is brought up through a hole from below, looped over the binder strip, run back into the same hole, then brought along under the seat frame to the next hole, brought up, looped over the binder strip, etc. (See Figures 4-19 and 4-20.)

STEP 8

Knots will not hold satisfactorily in plastic cane, so I use a peg system to permanently anchor the many ends of cane. Whittle pegs from scrap cedar so they will fit snugly in the holes.

Drive the pegs from the top to anchor the cane in the four corner holes and break them off. Punch the pegs down a little farther so they will be below the surface of the seat frame. Now turn the seat over and with nippers cut off the loose ends of cane in the corner holes only. (See Figure 4-21.)

Remember not to cut off any loose ends at any time until the cane is permanently pegged!

The rest of the permanent anchoring is done from the bottom of the seat. You only have to anchor those holes with loose ends of cane. Drive the pegs tightly into the holes, but not too far in to avoid disrupting the lay of the cane on the face of the seat. Break off the pegs as you go and then trim the loose cane off flush. (See Figures 4-22 and 4-23.)

Once the pegging is complete, mix a little epoxy and thicken it to the consistency of peanut butter. From the underside of the seat, dab epoxy into the pegged holes to lock everything together.

Fitting the Seat in the Boat

When the epoxy has set up, lay the seat where it belongs in the boat and, with a pair of dividers or a compass, mark the extended side arms of the seat for proper fit. Cut the ends carefully with a handsaw, sand them to soften the raw edges, and then touch up the

bare wood with a coat of varnish.

When the varnish has dried, cut small squares of felt and stick them on the bottom of the seat frame where it touches the sides of the boat and the seat stringer. Stick-on felt is available from most hardware stores and is perfect for preventing squeaks, which can be annoying when paddling.

Now fasten the seat to the seat stringer with two 1 ¾-inch stainless or bronze screws, drilled and countersunk. (See Figure 4-24.)

If you will be paddling only for an hour or so at a time, the caned seat is comfortable and cool on its own. If you will be paddling all day, or even for a half day, a piece of foam on top of the seat can make it easier on your tailbone. I use a heavy piece of corrugated foam mattress left over from a hospital stay. For even more comfort, many people use a Crazy Creek chair designed for canoes; it is supplemented with a Therm-A-Rest mattress, which can double as a sleeping aid when camping.

For real comfort, an adjustable footrest is important. I use a 16-inch length of dowel or bamboo, with a piece of line at each end that ties off to the seat or the rails on each side. (See Figure 4-25.) This system is infinitely adjustable, it is simple, it is lightweight, and it works.

Figure 4-18: The second diagonal strip has been woven, revealing the finished pattern of the seat, complete with binder strip.

Figure 4-19: The binder strip is held in place with lacing looped over the top.

Figure 4-20: The binder strip is secured by pulling the lacing taut from below.

Figure 4-21: Nipping off the loose ends of cane in the corner hole from the underside of the seat.

Figure 4-22: Pegging the loose ends from under the seat.

Figure 4-23: The loose ends pegged and trimmed off.

Figure 4-24: The cane seat fastened to the seat stringer. The piece of bamboo fastened with light line to the inner rails is the footrest.

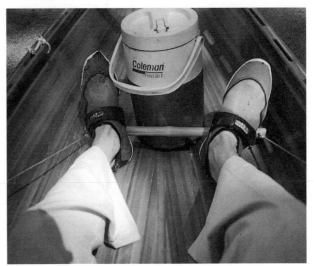

Figure 4-25: The footrest in action.

CHAPTER FIVE

Varnishing

There are two reasons to varnish your boat: (1) A cured epoxy surface is not perfect; rather, it is slightly rippled and dimpled, and must be sanded smooth and given a proper coating, and (2) ultraviolet rays have an adverse effect on epoxy and the wood under it. To protect our investment in time and material we must take the time to coat our little craft with UV-inhibiting varnish. This is when the Wee Lassie really starts to shine.

The shine, by the way, is a very important part of UV protection, so when your boat has lost its gloss, it is time to revarnish.

I always wait at least three days after the last coat of epoxy has been applied before I varnish. I prefer to wait a week. This allows any vapors or chemicals to do their thing, and a final cure to take place. If you varnish too soon, the varnish may not harden properly.

Make sure your varnish and the epoxy you used don't have a problem with each other. Try a sample if in doubt. I have had excellent results through the years with Captain's Varnish and Flagship Varnish, both by Z-Spar; I now use Flagship. Both brands work well with West System epoxy and 207 hardener. I stay away from the linear polyurethane varnishes. Though they produce a beautiful, hard surface, they are extremely expensive, extremely toxic, and very difficult for the amateur to apply properly.

Scratch Resistance

If you like to explore, you are bound to scratch the hull on oyster bars or gravelly beaches. I coat the bottom of my canoes with several coats of epoxy with a special powder additive before I varnish. (See Figure 5-1.) The powder is part of the West System and is intended to be a barrier coating to increase the waterproofness of their epoxy. At the same time, it increases the scratch resistance. I have paddled over oyster bars where I could hear the shells grating against the bottom with hardly any noticeable damage. I recommend using this additive on any hull that will be seeing similar hard usage.

Applying epoxy with barrier powder is not difficult. Simply outline the area you want to protect with masking tape. Sand the prior coat of epoxy for a good bond, mix the epoxy and the hardener, and add the powder to the mixture. Use a spreader to apply the epoxy and then roll it out as smoothly as you can. This coating usually requires two coats to hide the wood grain completely; it has a neutral gray color when it dries. Make sure you pull the masking tape while the coating is still tacky, otherwise the tape can be very difficult to remove.

Preparation

Preparation is the most important aspect when varnishing. You can use the best varnish, the best brushes, and the best brushing technique, and you can still get a rotten finish if you skimp on the preparation work.

Preparation is one of the main reasons why I apply more coats of epoxy to the surface of the boat than is required for strength. There must be enough epoxy over the fiberglass cloth to allow the epoxy to be sanded to a perfectly smooth finish without getting down to the fiberglass cloth or down to such a thin layer of epoxy over the cloth that the cloth will print through in time. There must also be a thick enough layer of epoxy left to provide a waterproof skin over the boat.

Sanding the epoxy smooth is a balancing act, best done with a random-orbit sander. Start with 80-grit paper, with the machine set at a medium speed. Carefully sand the hull until there are no bright spots left. You are looking for a matte finish, with no shiny dimples. Be especially careful at the bow and stern where the bias strips of fiberglass cloth were applied; try to get these areas as smooth as possible without sanding into the cloth itself.

You may find depressions that need filling with epoxy to achieve a fair surface. If there are too many of these areas, it might be smart to recoat the hull with another coat of epoxy, or even two, and then resand. This is a judgment call. You must balance how quickly you want to be done and in the water against how perfect you want the boat to be.

When all is sanded and the surface is fair, resand lightly with 120-grit paper. Again, the more bright, shiny spots you eliminate by sanding, the better your varnish job will be. Varnish does not hide a poor sanding job. Rather, it highlights one. Believe me.

When the surface has been properly prepared, set up the canoe where it will not be exposed to sunlight or airborne dust and vacuum it well. Then remove any sanding residue with a tack cloth, which can be obtained at any paint store and which can really help in producing a good varnish job. I never use a tack cloth between coats of epoxy for fear of contamination, but I always use it before any coat of varnish.

Application

I use a 3-inch foam brush to apply varnish. Unless you varnish all the time, I feel that the money spent on a good varnish brush and the solvents required to take care of it would be wasted.

Fill the brush with varnish and lay it on the hull. Work the varnish in an up-and-down, overlapping pattern, then tip off toward the wet area, working lengthwise with the grain of the wood. Start at one end of the hull and work right around the boat, always tipping off toward the finished area to avoid a cold joint.

If you just brush on the varnish in one direction, you will probably get holidays (bare spots) or, worse yet, runs. You want to avoid such imperfections, especially runs, as they do not dry hard and are very difficult to sand out. By brushing up and down to spread the varnish, and then lightly tipping off lengthwise, you can avoid both of these problems.

Allow the varnish to dry at least overnight before sanding lightly in preparation for the next coat. I use a palm sander with 220-grit paper for this light sanding. Again, use a tack cloth to get rid of any dust before recoating.

Revarnish, lightly sand, revarnish... three or four coats, inside and out, does the job.

As the years go by and scratches appear in the finish, a light sanding and another coat of varnish will restore the canoe to its original appearance. Gradually, as time passes, a deep, rich patina will be achieved.

Stephen Poe has owned one of my canoes for over twelve years now. He brings it to the Wooden Canoe Heritage Assocation assembly each year, where I see it, and although he uses it more than any of his other canoes it still looks brand-new because he has maintained it carefully. The boat probably has had 16 coats of varnish, and the surface looks like glass.

Figure 5-1: A sailing canoe finished with a barrier coating to increase abrasion resistance.

Use three or four coats of varnish, inside and out.

There is something special about Merchants Millpond. I consider this jewel to be one of the hidden wonders of North Carolina. Its setting is the gently rolling farmland in the northeast corner of the state. It is easy to miss the turnoff to the pond, although it is marked. The country road curls around a wooded area, and suddenly you catch glimpses of the water.

Every time I have been on the pond, the surface has been solid duckweed, but I notice the trees first. It is as if God created a pond and decided there was too much glare, so He took up a handful of cypress- and gum-tree seeds and scattered them over the surface of the water. Where the seeds landed, they grew and flourished. The result is a forest to paddle through.

Trees are scattered in big bunches and in individual clusters. The duckweed carpets the surface of the water in vast areas and rustles as you paddle through it. When you hit uncovered water, you feel as if your canoe has slipped loose; the rustling stops and the silence deepens, and you glide through water that is the color of strong, black coffee.

There are turtles in great numbers in Merchants Millpond, and great blue herons. There are Canada geese and ducks if the time of year is right. And there are mink, their fur glistening as they climb out of the water onto a stump.

At the far end of the pond you paddle into Lassiter Swamp and everything changes. Here, as the feeder stream winds slowly through a cypress forest, it is dark. Many of the trees are warped and twisted, with heavy burls caused by parasitic mistletoe, and there are water moccasins. This would make a perfect setting for a horror movie.

A steady succession of beaver dams crosses the stream. These dams and a fear of getting lost in the swamp have discouraged me from going deeper in, but I hear there are truly enormous cypress trees back there. These trees escaped the loggers and have been here since long before Columbus's time.

I have only paddled Merchants Millpond in the

summer. Usually I am there during the week, and normally I spend most of the day exploring. I might see one other boat. I understand that in cooler weather the pond is more heavily used; it must be gorgeous on a cool autumn day. There is a canoe camping area on one side of the pond, as well as a family campground nearby. The parking area at the pond is safe, so you don't have to worry about vehicle security while you are out paddling.

My usual route to Merchants Millpond is to turn off US 95 at Roanoke Rapids and travel east on Route 158. It is about an hour and half drive from the interstate. The turnoff to the park is between Gatesville and Sunbury.

I am usually on my way north when I stop at Merchants Millpond. On most trips, after enjoying the pond, I continue east on Route 158 to Route 17, head north to the bridge-tunnel system across the mouth of Chesapeake Bay, then explore my way up the Delmarva Peninsula. There is an excellent park with camping and good canoeing at Trapp Pond State Park, and another great pond, Trussum, to explore nearby. You won't find any powerboats at Trussum or Merchants Millpond, but you will find them at Trapp Pond.

How I judge a stream or pond is subjective — the weather the day I was there, a feeling of solitude, or a lack of solitude — but the places I mention in this book are the places I go back to year after year. To me they all rate more than ten on a scale of ten.

Some of the places I really like would bore paddlers looking for excitement or a stretch of uncomplicated water to see how far they can go on a particular day. My style of paddling is more like taking a stroll, where there is no hurry, no time limit, and no destination. Just a leisurely exploration through a different world.

I definitely stop to smell the roses. Sometimes I shut my eyes and just drift, and listen to the silence. A silence composed of distant bird calls, winds whispering through treetops, insects rubbing their wings together. I empty my brain, stop thinking, and just am. What a great way to spend a summer afternoon.

BACK TO WORK

CHAPTER SIX

Making a Double Paddle

You should start making your double paddle before you finish the canoe itself. It would be a shame to have the boat ready to launch and not have an elegant paddle to go with it. You wouldn't want to have to throw something together at the last minute. A closet pole with two plywood disks for blades doesn't go well with a beautifully finished little canoe.

You might also like to make a small single-bladed paddle and keep it tied under the seat of your canoe. This can be made from a scrap piece of cedar or spruce and is very handy when you are exploring tight waterways, such as the mangrove tunnels in my home waters, and have no room to use a double paddle.

Paddle Design

Having a well-designed paddle makes a big difference in the performance of your canoe. One lady I made a paddle for compared it to the bow used to play a violin. She had recently shopped for a bow for her son's violin and was amazed to hear the difference in tone produced by bows of differing quality. The same applies to paddles.

I like my paddle to be as light in weight as possible, with a little spring or flex in the shaft. There is no sense in having a light canoe and using a heavy club for a paddle.

A double paddle can be light and flexible, because it usually doesn't have to take the abuse that a regular paddle does. As the motion of the double paddle is more like that of an oar — the blade stays close to the surface of the water — the blade is less apt to become jammed between rocks or roots. A single-bladed paddle, which is thrust deeply in the water, isn't so lucky.

A canoeist paddling for speed must dig the blade deeply into the water, using more of a windmill style than I do. I tend to mosey along, bringing my blade out of the water on one side just far enough to immerse the blade on the other side. The farther up you lift the blade, the more energy is expended, and the more water tends to run down the blade, over the turkshead, and into your boat, or down the shaft to your hands. If your hands are wet all the time, they might blister. Under normal cruising conditions my hands stay dry.

Many old Eskimo kayaks had a paddle rest directly in front of the paddler to carry the weight of the paddle. The paddler's effort went into propulsion, not holding up the paddle. The Eskimo's paddle was very long and narrow-bladed, about as far from the contemporary wing paddle design as you can get.

The design of my paddle blade lies somewhere between the narrow blades of the Eskimos and the wide blades of some of the present-day commercial double paddles. My blade is long but a little wider than the Eskimo quill. In use, it is the quietest paddle I have found, and quiet is what I desire more than speed. (See Figure 6-1.)

My paddle is quite traditional in design. L. Francis Herreshoff, Pete Culler, and quite a few of the late-19th-century builders, such as J. Henry Rushton and W.P. Stephens, used the same basic design. Mr. Stephens's book *Canoe and Boat Building for Amateurs*, published in 1889, shows four or five typical designs; he suggests a blade 6 to 7 inches wide and 18 to 20 inches long, with a shaft diameter of 1 1/4 inches.

There are two basic blade orientations on a double paddle: feathered, where the blades are set at right angles to each other, or nearly so; and unfeathered, where the blades lie on the same plane. (See Figure 6-2.) I usually recommend an unfeathered paddle for the beginner, as it is simpler to build and to learn to use than a feathered paddle.

The theory behind the feathered paddle is that the blade in the air creates less wind resistance, as its edge is oriented forward. To make the paddle work properly, however, the paddler must twist his wrist on each stroke and, for some people, this can lead to tendonitis. For this reason, most long-distance paddlers seem to prefer the unfeathered type.

Feathered or unfeathered — the choice boils down to whatever you get used to and feel comfortable with. After all, it is your boat and your paddle.

I recommend a spoon-shaped blade, because I believe it is more efficient than a flat blade. A spoon-bladed paddle isn't that much more difficult to make than the flat type, and it certainly looks elegant.

The length of the paddle is determined by the width of your boat, although your height affects the length, too. For the Wee Lassie, most people seem to prefer an 8-foot paddle, but if you are over 6 feet tall, a paddle 6 inches longer would be fine. A 9-footer is the longest paddle I feel comfortable using.

Getting Started

Find a piece of straight, clear spruce; a 1 by 6 will do. For an 8-foot paddle you will need a 12-foot length to have material for the shaft and enough left over for the blades.

Or, you could make the shaft of spruce, which is quite light in color, and the blades of cedar, which is darker. This won't make the paddle work any better, but it will provide a striking visual effect. I do not recommend using heavy hardwoods for the blades, however; keep the paddle as light as possible.

Cut the spruce board to the overall length of the paddle, then rip it on a table saw so you will have two 1 1/2-inch-wide pieces, 3/4 inch thick. These pieces should be clear, without knots or flaws; they will be glued together to make the shaft.

Cut the leftover 4-foot piece into two 2-foot pieces. Make a simple template from the paddle plan and use it to lay out six curved pieces, which will be glued together for the blades, on each of these 2-footers. (See Figure 6-3.) Cut out these laminations with a sabersaw or bandsaw. (If you want to make your paddle a little fancier, you can use strips of mahogany or walnut between the laminations.)

Use one of these curved pieces as a pattern to mark the shape of the ends of the long pieces that will become the shaft and, with a sabersaw or bandsaw, cut away the waste. (See Figure 6-4.)

Gluing Up the Paddle

If you still have it, use the building board you built your boat on for a gluing platform; otherwise, use a long bench.

Glue up the paddle with catalyzed epoxy thickened with colloidal silica to the consistency of thick honey. Use a throwaway brush to spread the mixture on all mating surfaces. Clamp everything together and let it set overnight before beginning to shape your paddle. I use four bar clamps to clamp

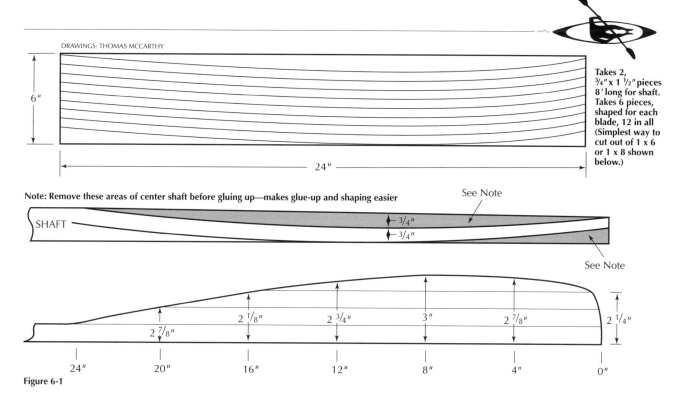

DRAWINGS: THOMAS MCCARTHY

6"

24"

Takes 2,
³/₄" x 1 ½" pieces
8' long for shaft.
Takes 6 pieces,
shaped for each
blade, 12 in all
(Simplest way to
cut out of 1 x 6
or 1 x 8 shown
below.)

Note: Remove these areas of center shaft before gluing up—makes glue-up and shaping easier

See Note

SHAFT

³/₄"
³/₄"

See Note

2 ⁷/₈"

2 ¹/₈"

2 ³/₄"

3"

2 ⁷/₈"

2 ¹/₄"

24"   20"   16"   12"   8"   4"   0"

Figure 6-1

Figure 6-2: A selection of double paddles of varying length and blade shape. The top paddle has feathered blades at 90 degrees. The middle paddle is feathered at 45 degrees and has a ferrule so the feather angle can be further adjusted and the paddle can be taken apart. The rest of the paddles are not feathered and cannot be taken apart.

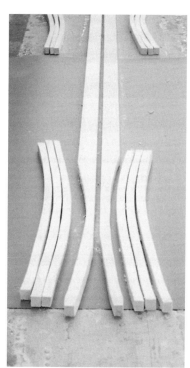

Figure 6-4: The curved laminations for the blade have been cut, as have the ends of the two pieces that will be glued together for the shaft. The same must be done for the other end of the double paddle.

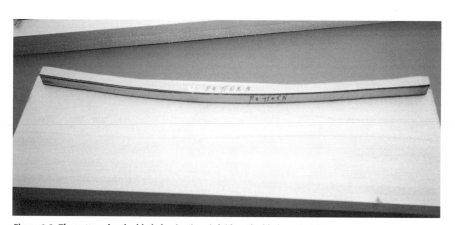

Figure 6-3: The pattern for the blade laminations is laid on the blade material.

each blade, and C-clamps every 6 inches along the shaft. (See Figure 6-5.)

Shaping the Blades

When the glue has cured, remove the clamps and, with a disc sander with a 24-grit disc, shape the power face — the concave-curved side — of each blade. (See Figure 6-6.) Any disc sander will do this job if you are careful. Use a light touch to give the blade face a nice fair curve. Shaping the power face first creates a good, clean surface on which to draw the outline of the blade.

After establishing the outline of the blade, trim it to shape with a sabersaw or bandsaw.

Now establish the thickness of the blade. Do this by drawing a pencil line all around the edge of the blade, $1/4$ inch away from the power face.

Using the glue line between the two shaft pieces as a centerline reference, use the disc sander to fair off the excess wood from the centerline of the back face of the blade out to the line you just drew to establish the thickness of the blade. Also with the sander, fair the shaft of the paddle into the back face of the blade, being careful to maintain the full thickness of the shaft at the centerline. (See Figure 6-7.)

Shaping the Shaft

I far prefer an oval shaft in cross section to a round one, as the feel of it in my hands always indicates the orientation of the blade, especially when bracing in rough water. The instructions here apply to such an oval shaft.

The glued-up shaft is at the moment $1 1/2$ inches square in section. Plane off approximately $1/8$ inch on each side perpendicular to the blades. The shaft becomes rectangular in section.

Draw lines along the shaft about $3/8$ inch in from the corners, on each side of each corner. With a hand plane, plane off the corners to the lines, making the shaft octagonal in cross section.

From here on, shaping the shaft is a matter of rounding and fairing until as much of the excess wood as possible is removed and the shaft feels right in your hands. A block plane is good for most of this, as is a spokeshave; either tool must be sharp and properly adjusted to be of any help. A gouge, also sharp, can be helpful in fairing the back of the blade into the shaft.

Finishing Off the Paddle

When the paddle — shaft and blades — is shaped to your satisfaction, smooth the surface with a random-orbit sander. Start with 36 or 40 grit, then drop down to 80 and 120 grit and follow up with hand sanding to remove any rough edges or tool marks.

If you have a woodburning tool, you can use it to draw designs — birds, animals, what have you — on the blades before they are sealed.

Seal the entire paddle with a coat of unthickened epoxy, allowing it to cure for several days.

The paddle is finished in the same way the hull was finished: Sand the epoxy for a smooth, fair surface, then give it several coats of varnish, sanding lightly between coats.

A turkshead knot at the neck between each blade and the shaft adds a nautical touch to the paddle and acts as a drip cup to help prevent water from running down the shaft onto your hands. A drip cup helps somewhat, but the best way to keep water away from your hands is to paddle properly. Most people who complain about water running back down the paddle shaft are digging the blade too deeply into the water, thus raising the opposite blade too high in the air.

You can reinforce the blades with fiberglass cloth if you desire, though doing so adds weight to the paddle, and too much weight can be tiring on a long trip. If you use your paddle properly, the reinforcement will not be necessary, but if you do decide to add fiberglass cloth, apply it to both sides of the blade.

A Take-Apart Paddle

If you want to take your paddle apart to make it easier to transport or to be able to change from a feathered to a nonfeathered configuration at will, you can cut it in half in the middle of the shaft and fit a ferrule to the now-independent parts.

I prefer a partially feathered paddle, set at about a 45-degree angle, rather than the more conventional 90 degrees. So far I have not been bothered by tendonitis. With a ferrule on a take-apart paddle, you can change the angle of the blades until you are comfortable, and then put four small screws through the ferrule into the shaft to retain the position you prefer. Since an 8-foot paddle will fit inside your canoe on top of your vehicle while traveling, I can see little advantage to a take-apart paddle other than the ability to feather or unfeather the blades.

The only time I take my paddle apart is when I am sailing my Feather canoe. I slide the two sections up on either side of the centerboard case, which keeps them out of the way while sailing, but lets me quickly put the paddle back together again if I want to drop the sail and commence paddling.

A metal ferrule for a take-apart paddle must be carefully machined to work properly, and machining is expensive. One simple way to get around this problem is to make the ferrule from a 10-inch piece of 1 ¼-inch PVC pipe, an inexpensive item at any hardware store. I have been using a PVC ferrule for over two years on my own paddle and have had no problems. It doesn't look as good as a brass ferrule, but it works, doesn't corrode, and is inexpensive. Not a bad combination.

To fit the ferrule, simply shape the end of one paddle shaft for a hard-drive fit into the PVC pipe, and then shape the other paddle half for a snug fit. (See Figure 6-8.)

Figure 6-6: The power face of the blade is shaped first.

Figure 6-5a (above) and Figure 6-5b (left): Glue is spread on the laminations and the entire assembly is clamped together at once: the two pieces for the shaft and the six pieces for the blade on each end.

Figure 6-7: The back of the blade is shaped with a disc sander.

Figure 6-8: For a take-apart paddle with a PVC-pipe ferrule, the end of one shaft is shaped for a hard-drive fit and the end of the other for a snug fit.

CHAPTER SEVEN

Using the Wee Lassie

Now that you have built your Wee Lassie, it is time to go paddling.

Dress according to the weather. The only special item I wear are shoes that protect the bottoms of my feet yet still allow the water to drain out. I never go barefoot anymore. Too many people like to break their soda and beer bottles overboard, rather than recycle them.

Getting Underway

I prefer to get underway from a clean, gently shelving beach. Such an ideal is not always available, but we'll assume that is what we have now. Put the Wee Lassie in the water, with the bow toward the shore and the stern toward deeper water. Put one foot in the center of the boat, forward of the seat, the double paddle crossways on the rails, then lower your posterior onto the seat; push off the beach with the other foot, then get it into the boat. This takes longer to describe than to do.

Getting into the boat from a dock is a little more difficult. The main thing is to get one foot in the center of the boat, then get your fanny down into the seat as soon as possible. Do not try to stand up in a Wee Lassie: if you do, you'll be going swimming.

Once you are seated and the paddle is in your hand, you can adjust the foot brace until it is comfortable. Use a float cushion against the thwart as a backrest. At this point, capsizing the boat is almost impossible.

The use of a double paddle is simple to learn.

Try to keep the shaft of the paddle as close to horizontal as possible. The motion is more like rowing facing forward than it is to paddling in the standard manner, where you dig the blade straight down into the water. Try to maintain a smooth and easy motion. I like to paddle quietly, working the blade so it enters the water without a splash and exits the same way.

To apply more power to your stroke, pull on the side of the paddle in the water and push with the other hand. If you want to add more power yet, you can use the rotation of your upper body in addition to arm motion. This brings into play more powerful muscles. A foot brace is a must when power-paddling, as it helps keep your body erect and in the proper position for taking a strong stroke.

On a long passage up a lake or a bay, I will use power strokes to keep my Wee Lassie at hull speed or above, but when I am exploring a narrow creek or a stream, my goal is simply to paddle along as quietly as possible, to avoid scaring the local wildlife. It is amazing what you will see if you slow down and take the time to look.

Exercise and the Wee Lassie

In the past, I felt that rowing a boat rigged with a sliding seat would provide just about the perfect exercise anyone could want. I would still hold that opinion, except for one point: I quickly lose my motivation to go rowing — all exercise and no fun.

While my rowing shell weighs about the same as my Wee Lassie, launching it takes three trips from the boathouse or car to the water. Once with the boat, once with the drop-in sliding seat, which is especially difficult to get into and out of a van, and once with the oars and lifejacket.

There are other disadvantages, too. A shell is stable only when the oars are rigged and are ready to use, or are being used. If equipment breaks — an oar, a rigger, an oarlock, a wheel on the sliding seat — you are quickly in trouble. Furthermore, you cannot go exploring in a shell, and traveling backwards can, on occasion, be dangerous to your health.

A Wee Lassie is simple. You have the boat and a double paddle. If the paddle should break, you can get home with half a paddle. (You cannot get home with half an oar, or even with one complete oar, unless you have a sculling socket.) You are facing forward, which means you can see your way through narrow and twisty passages.

Because a Wee Lassie can get into places no other boats are likely to go, you can have more fun closer to home. Any stream or pond is fair game for exploration. With a shell, you must have open water, and that can be boring.

The Wee Lassie offers me a much wider selection of places to paddle close to my shop, and I therefore tend to use it much more often than I use my shell. Frequent exercise out in the fresh air is more beneficial, I feel, than the occasional use of a rowing shell, even though the quality of the exercise might be better in the shell. This is one of those few times when quantity, or frequency, is better than quality.

Places to Paddle

When people ask me where to use a Wee Lassie, I tell them any place they can see water. You don't have to paddle all day to enjoy yourself, and you don't have to wait all year for a vacation to enjoy wilderness. Usually, no matter where you live — the United States, Canada, South Africa, wherever — there is at least a nearby small stream or a pond waiting to be explored.

In even the largest metropolitan areas, you can still find places to enjoy a small, lightweight canoe. As I mentioned in the introduction to this book, here in Sarasota, Florida, there are good paddling waters within minutes of my shop. On Lido Key, with high rises visible above the mangroves, you can paddle through a miniature Everglades, with mangrove tunnels, quiet lagoons, and rookery islands.

A little farther up the bay is Whitaker Bayou, which runs back into an older section of town. It has been heavily polluted and abused, but if you close your eyes to the occasional clutter of trash on the banks, such as grocery carts and old tires, you can feast your eyes on gorgeous old oak trees and backyard gardens. The herons don't seem to mind the clutter, and large mullet will swirl the water ahead of your canoe. There are surprises around each bend, including low bridges and culverts.

Waters like these are not heavily traveled. You will have left the motorboats behind; early in the morning the atmosphere is quiet and peaceful.

There's peaceful paddling water in the unlikeliest places. In Washington, D.C., I have seen fox on their way through the parking lot of the C & O Canal. The canal itself seems more like a river. The banks are overgrown with wildflowers in bloom; from across the towpath you can hear the reason for the canal: the Potomac River, smashing through raw rock, on its way to

Chesapeake Bay.

North of Baltimore, Deer Creek, which is known for its whitewater, has an excellent, if small, section of flat water, backed up by a milldam. A little farther south, but still north of Baltimore, I have paddled a reservoir and seen heron and muskrats.

Below Washington, an hour east of I-95 from Roanoke Rapids, is Merchants Millpond, an enchanted body of water covered with emerald-green duckweed, studded with great cypress and bay trees. You feel as if you are paddling through an open forest, with constantly changing vistas ahead of the canoe. Here there are mink, beaver, herons, osprey, and numerous ducks. The sound of your paddle is the only noise to break the summer stillness.

On the Eastern Shore of Chesapeake Bay, you can camp at Trapp Pond and paddle there, or visit another tiny, secret place nearby, Trussum Pond. For that matter, you could spend your entire lifetime in the Chesapeake region and not have enough time to paddle all the rivers, creeks, streams, coves, and bays.

There is great paddling all over the Adirondacks, but the farther north you go, the better. By the time you have reached the St. Regis area, you will have left most of the jet skis behind. But anywhere you go, once you have portaged your canoe around a beaver dam, things will be quieter.

The paddling is great in Northern Vermont and the Connecticut Lakes area of New Hampshire. The inlets are more interesting than the lakes themselves and are more protected from the winds.

In Maine, the Rangeley, Dover-Foxcroft region provides wonderful canoeing for a small boat. And down on the coast, the protected bays and inlets can be great fun if you are careful with the tides and watch out for the fog. Common sense is the rule here. Poking around a small Maine harbor can be an enjoyable experience if you just love to look at boats, as I do. I don't care how big they are, or how small, workboat or yacht, all boats fascinate me.

There is good canoeing water everywhere. Someday, I want to explore the Midwest, and Louisiana, and Oregon, and Alaska....

But in the meantime I really am quite content as long as I can spend a couple of early mornings a week prowling the shores of Sarasota Bay, or paddling the Myakka River just east of town.

Sailing the Wee Lassie

Sailing the Wee Lassie is fun, and if all you want to do is sail downwind, it can be simple: all you need is an umbrella. No boat can sail directly into the wind even with a sail more elaborate than an umbrella, but with a leeboard, or a centerboard, you should be able to sail as close as 45 or 50 degrees to the wind, which will get you home if the tide isn't running against you.

A great deal of pleasure is to be derived from leaning back against the thwart and letting a small sail do the work for awhile. It doesn't take a lot of sail area to move a small canoe, and because your weight is low in the boat, you really have more stability than most people would think.

But modifying a canoe for sailing does add weight and complexity, so you may want to proceed cautiously. To see if you will enjoy canoe sailing, you can temporarily modify your boat with a mast partner and step.

The maststep is a simple block of wood with a hole in it to take the heel of the mast. It is epoxied to the inside bottom of the boat on the centerline. Likewise, the mast partner is another simple piece of wood, with a hole in the center to accept the mast. This can be clamped to the rails, rather than permanently installed.

The Wee Lassie is suitable for protected water anywhere.

I prefer the rig as shown in Figure 7-1, because it is so simple — one halyard to raise or lower the sail; one sheet to control the sail. I like to be able to drop the sail instantly if the boat becomes too hard pressed, or to let the sheet run free so the air will be spilled from the sail. Both of these maneuvers are safety features and allow you to revert to double paddling quickly and simply if the wind starts to blow too hard for comfort, or if you get tired of tacking against a tide.

The sailing rig shown in Figure 7-1 is only one of many choices, however. There is a wide variety of small-craft rigs that will work on the Wee Lassie, from a simple lugsail to a fancy windsurfer rig. For my rig, I make the spars from bamboo, as it is light and very strong, and the mast from spruce. If you can't find bamboo, spruce will do just fine for the spars.

Rather than cut a centerboard slot in the bottom of your canoe right at the start, first try a simple leeboard. Use one that just hooks over the rail and is held in place by a bungee cord. Use your paddle to steer, and wear a life jacket. You will know soon enough whether or not you like sailing your little craft.

If you find you really like to sail, you might want to cut a slot in the bottom of the boat and replace the leeboard with a centerboard or daggerboard. I prefer a centerboard, because it pivots up when it touches bottom. A daggerboard can bring you to a dead stop, which can cause damage to the daggerboard case and/or the boat.

A leakproof centerboard case is easily added to your canoe. Basically, the case is just a long, narrow box without a top or bottom, in which the centerboard can pivot up and down. A slot is cut in the bottom of the boat, the bottom of the centerboard case is scribed to fit the bottom of the boat and cut to shape, and then the case is epoxied and glassed in place. The centerboard can be laminated from several pieces of wood, or it can simply be a piece of $1/2$-inch marine plywood. I drill holes in the bottom of the centerboard and fill them with lead, which weighs the board down and allows it to be raised and lowered with a simple lanyard. (Without weight, you can use a pivoting lever to force the board down and hold it in place.)

A single paddle is sufficient for steering the canoe, but a rudder is more convenient. I always make rudders with a drop-down blade, weight them like the centerboard, and control them with a push-pull tiller attached to a quadrant on the rudderhead. I fit the rudder with shock cord so it will be automatically centered when I am not pulling or pushing on the tiller.

I strongly recommend that you follow these simple safety rules when sailing your canoe: Always wear an approved life jacket. Learn to sail in shallow water, and on a nice day. When you get underway, keep in mind when and how you will return. The best plan is to sail against the wind on the way out, and come back with the wind behind you.

Sailing a tiny boat like this is an excellent way to learn to sail. You get very quick results from any action, whether it is right or wrong.

I find sailing my Wee Lassie to be like using a computer. Time literally flies, because I am concentrating totally on what I am doing. If the wind is just right, and the sun is warm, nothing can be more enjoyable or relaxing than a pleasant sail in a Wee Lassie around a small pond, lake, or bay.

Not much sail area is required.

All the controls are near at hand.

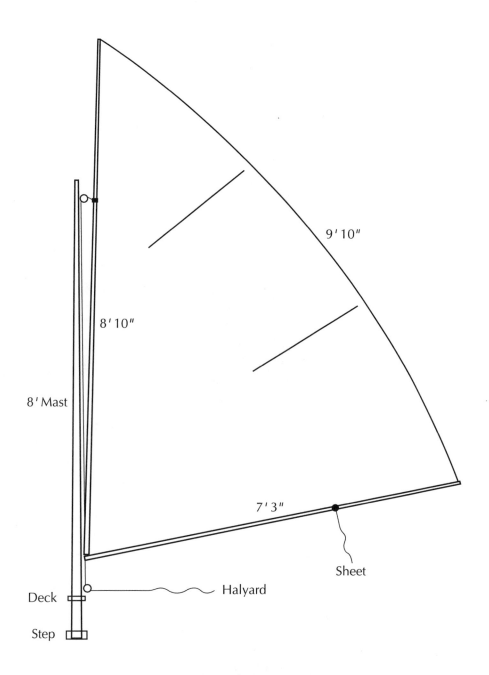

9′10″

8′10″

8′ Mast

7′3″

Sheet

Halyard

Deck

Step

Mast 1 ¹/₂″ spruce tapered to 1″ at top
Boom 1″ round spruce or bamboo
DRAWING: THOMAS MCCARTHY

Figure 7-1: Sail Plan for the Wee Lassie

On my drives north I try to avoid the major population centers, mainly the area from Washington, D.C., to above New York City. It takes longer to go the way I do, but the drive is more comfortable. From the Eastern Shore of Chesapeake Bay I drive north to Fallston in Maryland, where I visit with my son, then up through York and Scranton and Utica, and into the Adirondacks.

When I was a boy my family used to vacation for two weeks in the summer at a camp on Tupper Lake. I can remember my dad taking me out early in the morning in a guideboat to look for deer. That is a special memory for me. We would come back in and go to the dining room to eat breakfast. The room was big and open, and made of stone and logs, and I can still smell the apple fritters. What a way to start a day when you are four or five years old.

You could spend the rest of your life canoeing in the Adirondacks. The area has everything: big, open lakes, little lakes, ponds, rivers, streams, bogs, and marshes. Whitewater fury, and quiet-water serenity. And tourists. And jet skis.

Over the years I have slowly built up a list of places away from the crowded areas where you can paddle in peace and quiet, and where primitive campsites are usually available during the week. Horseshoe lake, just below Tupper Lake, is just such a place. The campsites are well spread out down one side of the lake, so you have visual and at least partial sound privacy. The lake is home to several loons, and

I have spent hours watching them through binoculars. If a loon doesn't wake me up sometime during the night, I feel cheated. To me their ghostly, agonizing calls are part of the mystique of camping out in the Adirondacks. The people who sleep in motels and lodges don't get the total experience at all.

Horseshoe Lake is a pleasure in and of itself, but it also makes an excellent location

to camp while trying out sections of the Bog River and the access area for Lows Lake. This is wilderness.

The St. Regis area is a mixture of wilderness, where you can portage from small pond to small pond, and civilization, where you can find larger lakes surrounded by

fabulous camps and boathouses. Exploring parts of Upper St. Regis Lake is like canoeing through a museum. The boathouses are full of restored runabouts, guideboats, and antique canoes. Nearby is another of my favorite spots, Buck Pond State Campground and Park.

Buck Pond itself is small, but no motorboats are allowed. It is great to slip a canoe into the water just before sunrise or just before sunset. I have usually been able to get a campsite right on the water. These campsites are not primitive, and they are close together with no visual or sound privacy. Loud radios, kids, and barking dogs can be distracting if what you have come for is peace and quiet, but all the regular campgrounds are like that. That's what I don't like about Buck Pond.

What I do like about Buck Pond is that a two-minute drive from your campsite is a launch area that provides access to Lake Kushaqua, Rainbow Lake,

Clear Pond, the North Branch of the Saranac River, and a flow area off Clear Pond. There are islands to explore, culverts full of swallows, beaver lodges, deer, and much bird life to observe and admire. There is motorboat traffic, but mostly fishermen, at least during the week. I imagine on a weekend motorboat traffic must increase substantially.

If you are on a pond, can't find peace and quiet, and want it, you can portage or carry to another pond. Motorboats don't portage well; featherweight canoes do. After several portages you will find peace and serenity, or at least kindred souls looking for the same.

BACK TO WORK

CHAPTER EIGHT

Thoughts on Strength and Weight

In this book we have been using the Wee Lassie canoe to illustrate the building techniques involved in the cedar-strip, epoxy-'glass system, which can be used to build a wide variety of small craft. I have used this method over the years to build many different types of canoes, rowing shells, sea kayaks, wave and surf skis, dinghies, and small sailboats.

While using sheet plywood is much simpler than laying strip planking on flat-bottomed hulls, I have used the cedar-strip system instead of plywood to save weight on several skiffs.

Another reason to go over to cedar strip is that plywood suitable for building a quality boat is getting difficult to find and becoming extremely expensive. Even some marine-grade plywood is full of voids and repaired imperfections; many sheets almost have to be remade to be usable. There are, therefore, advantages in quality, weight, and cost in using the cedar strip and fiberglass system rather than fiberglass-covered plywood on flat- or V-bottom craft.

One of the major advantages of the cedar-strip system is that you can vary the strength and weight of the boat simply by increasing or decreasing the thickness of the strips, and the weight of the cloth that you use inside and out. In engineering terms, using thicker cedar strips is the same as widening the web of an I-beam; the farther the inside and outside layers of glass cloth are separated, the stiffer the hull of the boat will be.

For instance, on a small sailboat, such as the traditional melonseed, I recommend using strips at least ⅜ inch thick and 6-ounce cloth. The melonseed has a flat area in the center of the bottom; here, I would recommend increasing the thickness of the strips to $\frac{1}{2}$ inch or $\frac{3}{4}$ inch. In addition, I usually overlap the 6-ounce cloth on the bottom area, plus add an extra piece over the flat, football-shaped area of the bottom, inside and out. That provides an almost bulletproof combination.

At the other end of the spectrum, I build rowing shells in which the weight is kept to an absolute minimum. I started rowing for exercise about ten years ago, and really enjoy it. Getting out three mornings a week to row for an hour or so seems to help clear out the epoxy fumes and wood dust from my lungs. With a drop-in outrigger and sliding-seat unit, all the hull of a rowing shell basically has to be able to do is maintain its shape and keep the water out. This means that the thickness of the strips can be reduced. For my shells, I use $\frac{3}{16}$-inch strips and use the same cove-and-bead bits to radius the edges as I use on $\frac{1}{4}$-inch strips.

I have used ribs of carbon tape to stiffen a hull; these seem to work well with very little addition in weight. To save even more weight, I use 2-ounce cloth, outside and inside, though I do add an extra layer under the area where the drop-in unit will fit, and deck over the hull with Styrofoam — it weighs next to nothing, yet increases flotation.

Saving Weight

There are several ways to make a small canoe lighter. One is to make it smaller. Naturally the smaller it is, the less material required to build it and therefore the lower the weight. But there is a limitation on size. The smallest boat I can use comfortably is the Sairy Gamp, which was originally designed and built by J. Henry Rushton back in the 19th century for the lightweight enthusiast Nessmuk (pen name for George Washington Sears). At a length of 9 feet 6 inches and a beam of only 26 inches, it is a great boat for someone who weighs in at a hundred pounds or less. I enjoy paddling my strip-planked version, but I do feel as if I am paddling a big lily pad. At 150 pounds, I am a little big for such a tiny craft. You have to be careful when you reduce size.

You can save weight in a boat by leaving off some or all of the amenities. You can build a boat with no decks or closed-off compartments, and use either an inner or an outer rail, but not both. Some people can happily live with such a boat, but many people who come into my shop for a lightweight canoe actually want all the conveniences of an ocean liner.

Weight can be saved by using lighter materials.

For example, spruce could be used for the rails of a canoe, rather than cherry or mahogany. Softwood rails, however, can be difficult to maintain. Dents caused by hitting a dock or from hard usage lead to cracked varnish and epoxy; moisture can get into the wood and cause discoloration and, possibly, rot.

The variety of wood used for the strip planking itself has a considerable affect on weight. I prefer Western red cedar, with Florida juniper running a close second. Both seem to offer the best ratio of strength to weight. Fir and hardwoods, such as mahogany, would certainly add strength to the hull, but they would also double the weight. Eastern white cedar is light and strong enough, if you can find it without a lot of knots; cypress is fine, but it is heavier.

Considering Strength

One of the main factors involving weight versus strength is how you intend to use your boat. If I row in open water that I know is clear of obstacles, I can get away with $\frac{3}{16}$-inch strips. But I use a canoe to go exploring. I run up on stumps, beaver dams, rocks, boulders, oyster bars, and all sorts of natural and man-made obstacles. I want a canoe that will be able to absorb these shocks and keep on going. Therefore, for my personal canoe and those I custom-build for other people (unless specified otherwise), I use $\frac{1}{4}$-inch-thick strips for the hull. If I were building a wide canoe, 36 inches or more, with a relatively flat bottom, I would go to $\frac{3}{8}$ inch strips.

Another way to control weight is in the selection of fiberglass cloth to cover the hull, inside and out. I use 4-ounce cloth almost exclusively on the Wee Lassie canoes, or any other types I build up to 16 feet long. This balances strength and weight in a sensible compromise. For canoes longer than 16 feet, I use 6-ounce cloth.

Always remember, however, that the heavier the cloth, the more epoxy will be required to fill the weave properly. This means the weight of the extra epoxy will be added to the extra weight of the cloth. (This works in reverse: reduce the weight of the cloth, and the weight of the epoxy used will be less, too.)

Weight can be reduced by cutting back on the number of coats of epoxy and varnish, but while each coat does add weight, it also prolongs the life of the boat. Which way to go is a judgment call; I prefer to err on the side of longevity and elegance.

When I first started building strippers, I built a canoe with fiberglass cloth on the outside only; the inside was sealed with epoxy but not cloth. I quickly found out that this was not the way to go, because it made a considerably weaker boat. What's more, the moisture content of the strip planking became unbalanced. Basically, the result — warping — was the same as if I had put Formica on one side of a cabinet door and not the other. The strips cupped, which created print-through on the outer surface, which could allow further moisture penetration and could have a serious, adverse effect on the longevity of the hull.

As mentioned above, I use 2-ounce cloth on the outside of my rowing shells, and you could certainly use this on a Wee Lassie, but it would affect the long-term durability of the hull. I have tried a compromise by using 2-ounce cloth on the inside of the hull and 4-ounce on the outside. This would seem to be sensible except for two factors:

(1) The inside of a canoe probably takes as much abuse as the outside, what with footgear covered with mud and sand, camping gear and camera boxes, and water sloshing around from rain and paddle drips.

(2) More importantly, laying 2-ounce cloth on the inside takes the patience of a saint. The cloth is so light that it tries to float on top of the epoxy and is extremely squirrelly to handle when wet. The end result is usually frustration, and a lot of air bubbles and wrinkles to sand out the next day. More epoxy will probably be used in covering the messed-up cloth than would have been used on 4-ounce cloth in the first place.

An effective way to cut down on the weight of a canoe is to cut down on your weight — not only the amount of gear you take with you, but also the weight of your body. Your body weight won't affect the weight of the canoe as far as carrying it is concerned, but the more you weigh, the more effort you will have to expend to paddle the canoe through the water and the stronger the canoe will have to be to absorb the shocks that will be augmented by your extra weight. A 100-pound person pushing down on the rails to get out of a canoe is one thing; a 200-pound person pushing down is a serious strain on any thwart or rail system.

The Bottom Line

Finally, here are my recommendations for building a lighter boat, if that is what you wish to achieve:

Use 4-ounce cloth, inside and out.

Carefully squeegee the epoxy so there will be no puddles, which will add weight if they are allowed to remain.

Eliminate any amenities you don't have to have.

Cut down on the size of the rails, decks, etc.

Eliminate a caned seat in favor of a simple foam cushion.

And after the boat has been built:

Keep down the weight of the gear and accessories you carry in the boat.

Reduce your body weight if you can.

A featherweight rowing shell.

The Sairy Gamp, even smaller than the Wee Lassie.

CHAPTER NINE

What Do I Do When...

I am halfway through spreading the epoxy on one side of the canoe, and the can is getting hot in my hand, and the epoxy seems to be thickening up a little. Do I pour it on, and try to spread it out really quickly?

No, No, No! Dump it. There is no way to save epoxy that is getting hot and has begun to thicken. Make sure what you already have on the boat is under control, and then mix up enough to finish the job.

This situation can be avoided by not mixing up more epoxy at any one time than you can handle comfortably. Have everything ready before you mix epoxy. Don't dillydally while you spread it, or micro-manage a small area; get it spread out on the hull as quickly as possible. Mixed epoxy in a can will heat up; epoxy on the boat will not go off as fast, giving you time to work it properly.

I sealed the wood with epoxy, and now I can see where I didn't sand well enough beforehand. The wood shows glue stains. What should I do?

There's not much you can do. You can't spot sand, or you will get discoloration. Either resand the entire hull, or live with the stains.

I have fiberglassed the entire boat and have put several coats of epoxy over the 'glass. Now I notice a cloudy discoloration in certain areas of the boat. Can I clear it up?

This was a common problem for me before I started using West System's 207 hardener, which is now the only hardener I allow in my shop. There is something in the other West System hardeners that combines with the moisture in the air under certain conditions and causes cloudiness at a later date.

The solutions are (1) to sand everything back to bare wood and start over again, (2) live with the problem, or (3) paint the hull. I have made several people cry when I gave them those choices, but there are no others.

You can't just peel off fiberglass that has been laid down with epoxy as you can if polyester resin had been used. Sanding epoxy and fiberglass cloth is a messy, itchy, annoying, unpleasant job. You might get the cloth to release with a heat gun, but I would not tackle a job like that for any amount of money.

I was sanding the hull on the inside, not paying attention to what I was doing. All of a sudden I saw daylight and realized I had sanded through the hull and almost through the 'glass on the exterior of the hull. What do I do now?

I have had students do this twice now — usually shortly after I told them not to sand sitting down, but to stand up and keep the sander moving.

The best solution is to finish sanding the hull, but before you seal the inside, mix up some epoxy and filleting blend, or wood dust, into a stiff paste, fill the bare spot and the surrounding area with the paste, and cover the repair with a small piece of scrap fiberglass cloth. Make sure the glass cloth is completely saturated. The next day sand this, and then seal the interior of the boat. Proceed with 'glassing the hull the following day.

The morning after I fiberglassed the boat, I noticed bubbles the size of dimes on the interior. Now what?

Be glad they aren't quarter size. Sand the entire interior well. The bubbles will turn white; this white area can be easily popped off with the point of a knife. (If you do not remove these white circles, the next coat of epoxy will seal them in there forever.) Sand the edges until no more white shows, vacuum the area, and mix up a single squirt of epoxy and hardener. Let this set up until it starts to thicken, and then use it to fill each depression. The following day sand everything again, and give the entire surface another coat of epoxy.

Air bubbles can be avoided in the first place by taking a little more care when 'glassing the interior of the boat. Check the boat before the epoxy has fully set up, and squeeze out with a gloved finger any air bubbles you see.

How often do I need to refinish my boat?

Frequency of refinishing depends on frequency of use. At the least, sand lightly once a year and revarnish. This is as much for U.V. protection as it is for aesthetics.

There are some deep scratches on the bottom of my boat. I think they go all the way through the fiberglass to the wood. What should I do?

These must be repaired immediately to keep water from penetrating the wood and causing rot. Let the boat dry well. Sand the area around the deep scratches and seal with epoxy. If the scratches are really bad, you might want to reinforce the area with scrap cloth. When the epoxy has had a chance to cure, sand again and revarnish.

I live in an area of oyster bars. Is there anything I can do to toughen up the bottom of my boat?

I toughen up the bottoms of my canoes with a barrier coating admixture. Before completely finishing the exterior of a canoe, tape off the perimeter of the bottom area where the boat is apt to be scratched deeply. Mix up enough epoxy to cover this area, usually about four squirts, and after stirring well, mix in colloidal silica and West System Barrier Coating. Make this mixture as stiff as mayonnaise, and use a spreader to cover the bottom area with it and a roller to even it out. Usually one coat is not enough to completely hide the wood, so wait until the coating is sticky to the touch, but nothing sticks to your finger, and lay on a second coat with a roller and finish with a foam brush. Let it set up a little, then pull the tape. Don't leave the tape on overnight, as it will become difficult to remove from under the set-up resin. The next day, sand the barrier coating smooth and apply one more full coat of epoxy before finish-sanding and varnishing.

Would it be better to use epoxy to glue the strips together, rather than carpenter's glue?

This would be overkill on a small boat, and I do not recommend it. With the epoxy and fiberglass coating, inside and out, no water should ever reach the strips or the carpenter's glue. To use epoxy would mean wearing gloves all the time you were stripping the canoe, and the mess to be cleaned up when you were done would be considerable. I know several people who used epoxy to strip a canoe, but they never did it again on later boats.

When I am making the transition from the side strips to the bottom strips, the inner stems get in the way. How do I work around them?

With a chisel, cut away the portion that is in your way. The main point is to make a neat transition of the side strips into the center bottom strip. You want a nice, gentle rocker in the bottom strip, with no humps or bumps. Shim a mold, or cut the mold a little if necessary.

I have trouble pulling the strips down tightly as I get up close to the tops of the inner stems. What can I do?

This is one of the reasons I shifted over to using nails through the strips into the molds, rather than $\frac{1}{2}$-inch staples. The Wee Lassie is not an easy craft to strip; use clamps, nails, and patience. Sometimes it pays to stop and let the glue set up well in the area you have already completed before continuing. Fortunately, there are only two or three strips that are difficult to pull into place.

I am having trouble cutting the strips into the center bottom strip. Any suggestions?

The best way I have found to do this job is to mark one end of the strip and then cut it. Put it in place, and recut it in place to make a neat fit. Then apply glue to the entire strip and lay it in place, clamping, or nailing and stapling, as you go. When you reach the far end, mark and cut this end in place. If there is a gap, and you are not a perfectionist, cut a sliver of wood to fill the gap; this will be difficult to see when you are finished. This is one job where the advantage of a Dozuki saw is obvious; it is an excellent tool for making nearly perfect joints.

By the time you get really good at doing this, your boat will be done.

The Adirondacks are great, but less-known areas in New Hampshire are, I believe, even better. I go almost to the Canadian border, all the way to the headwaters of the Connecticut River, and take up residence for a night or two at Deer Mountain Campground. Fresh drinking water comes from a pipe out by the road. There is no spigot, the water just comes out, ice cold, and runs off down the ditch along the side the road. The rest of the facilities are just as primitive. The campground has never been crowded when I was there, and it is close to Third Lake, and the East Inlet to Second Lake.

A slow paddle around the entire shoreline of Third Lake, plus the exploration of the outflow at least as far as the beaver dams, takes a couple of hours. There is no development except for a ramp just off the road, and I have always seen loons and families of ducks. The shoreline is pretty, lined with large rocks. Mountains surround the lake, and the heavy forest runs right down to the water. In a way it is like canoeing in a little cup. There is a pebble beach at the north end of the lake, and usually I go

for a swim there before returning to the truck.

I went to East Inlet early one morning. It was daylight, but the mist was still coming off the water. The put-in was like a shallow pond, with heavily forested shores. Everything suggested moose country, as I imagine parts of Canada to be. The locals even call the region Moose Alley. I've seen moose alongside the road. There are signs all over to beware of hitting them with your car. I thought it was like the manatees in Florida, that the state was worried about people killing the moose with their cars. Instead I finally realized it was the other way around. The signs were warning people that the moose wouldn't get out of the way, and as a result a lot of cars were being wrecked and people were being hurt.

I paddled East Inlet for over four hours. I saw many deer, many different kinds of ducks, several loons, but no moose. I would still call the inlet a fifteen on a scale of ten.

I finally saw my first moose in the water, doing what moose are supposed to do, in Maine. Actually, it was a mother moose and her calf. I had gone past the Rangeley Lake area, which was a little too crowded for my taste, and had stopped at a tiny campground on Gilman Pond that I had read about in the AMC *Quiet Water Canoe Guide* for Maine. The entrance to the campground is easy to miss going east on the little country road in front;

the sign is only visible from the other direction.

I had the place all to myself, with a site about 10 feet from the water. The gentleman and his wife who own the campground don't seem to encourage business; I think they like it best when no one is there. I spent an enjoyable evening talking with them.

Most of Gilman Pond is shallow, with many

stumps at the north end that discourage powerboats. My kind of place. The south end of the pond is more like a river, and there I saw my mother moose and her calf. They were belly deep in the water, eating water lilies. Mama moose pretty much ignored my approach, but baby moose got nervous. When he got nervous, so did I. I had visions of mama moose charging through the shallow water and trampling me and my little canoe into a bloody froth. I retreated a bit and snapped some pictures. With no telephoto lens, the moose didn't show up too well when I developed the pictures, but at least I could prove I saw not one, but two moose.

I left them to their dinner and continued down the arm of the pond. When I came back they were gone, but I felt fulfilled. For that reason, I would call

Gilman Pond a ten out of ten, at least. Small, but intimate, it was fun to explore. Nice campground. Pleasant memories.

I could go on and on. Every place I go I find wonderful places to paddle my small canoe. Now that you have your own featherweight canoe, you will, too. And one of the nicest aspects of your travels will be this:

When people look at your canoe and ask, "Did you build that?" you can say, "Yes, I sure did."

BACK TO WORK

Materials and Costs

Materials for the Wee Lassie

- One 4 x 8 sheet of $\frac{1}{2}$-inch particle board or $\frac{1}{2}$-inch regular plywood.
- Enough 1 x 4s and 2 x 4s to build a strongback and horses.
- At least fifty strips of $\frac{1}{4}$-inch by $\frac{3}{4}$-inch Western red cedar. You should be able to get this out of three 1 x 8s, 12 feet long, depending on the quality of the material.
- One quart Elmer's Carpenter's Glue.
- Three ounces, 1 $\frac{1}{4}$-inch, No. 18 headed nails.
- One roll masking tape.
- One piece of spruce 1 x 6, 12 feet long, for the paddle, inner stems, and feature strips.
- One piece of cherry or mahogany 1 x 6, 12 feet long, for the rails, thwart, and seat frames.
- One gallon West System epoxy resin; one-third gallon West System 207 hardener.
- Ten yards of 4-ounce fiberglass cloth, 50 inches wide. (This is a standard package from West System.)
- One small container of colloidal silica.
- One small container of barrier coating.
- One quart spar varnish. (I prefer Flagship brand varnish.)
- One small skein of common plastic cane.
- Five or six 1-inch throwaway brushes.
- Twelve 3-inch foam brushes.
- Four roller covers.
- Box of toothpicks.
- Six spreaders.
- Box of throwaway gloves (50).

Cost of Building a Wee Lassie (1996)

Basic hull
1" x 8" x 12' cedar planks, 3 @ $30	$90

Paddle
1" x 6" x 12' spruce, 1 @ $24	$24

Rails and seat
1" x 6" x 12' mahogany or cherry, 1 @ $35	$35
Fiberglass cloth, 4 oz., 10 yards	$100
#105 West System epoxy resin, 1 gal.	$68
#207 West System hardener, $\frac{1}{3}$ gal.	$50
	$367

The above does not include the cost of tools, the material for the strongback and the molds, and such miscellaneous items as sanding discs, staples, glue, foam brushes, roller covers, varnish, etc. I have not included a complete price list for two reasons: (1) Some builders might wish to use first-class plywood for the molds, and others might use scrap gleaned from a local building site; and (2) prices for the odds and ends necessary to the job will vary from region to region and store to store.

Many of the odds and ends, such as plastic resin spreaders and stick-on sanding discs, can be obtained from an auto paint store, sometimes at better prices than at a marine supply store.

A realistic cost in 1996 for the materials to build the Wee Lassie is in the neighborhood of $500. Some builders spend less than $300; some will spend more than $500. Whatever the final cost, you will be getting the most boat and the best quality paddling for the buck.

Materials for the Wee Lassie Two

All of the above for the standard Wee Lassie, with the following adjustments:

- Two 4 x 8 sheets, instead of one, $\frac{1}{2}$-inch particle board or $\frac{1}{2}$-inch regular plywood.
- For the strips and the rails, substitute 14-footers for the 12-footers.
- One extra 1 x 6 piece of Western red cedar for the strips.
- The 10-yard roll of fiberglass cloth specified above will just barely cover the boat; be careful not to waste any when you roll it out on the exterior of the hull.

Tools

I recently received a letter from a gentleman who said he had spent a bundle building his Wee Lassie, mainly because he didn't have any tools when he started and had a pretty complete workshop when he was done. In all honesty, I must say that it is quite difficult to build a Wee Lassie, or anything else, if you don't have the proper tools. Therefore, unless you already own a complete tool kit, you will be spending more money for tools than for building materials.

Keep in mind that you can save a lot of money by buying used tools. Also keep in mind that you want quality used tools that have not been abused. Keep your eyes open at garage sales, and watch the classified ads.

Table Saw

In my opinion, a table saw is the most essential tool for building the boats described in this book. Not only can you rip the strips, thus saving a lot of money, but also you can rip the rails, the stock for the inner and outer stems, etc. An expensive table saw isn't necessary unless you intend to build a lot of boats, or to build furniture or cabinets when you have finished building your canoe. Makita and Delta offer self-contained saws for under $300. Watch the classified ads; you might be able to pick up a used saw at a really good price.

The size of a table saw is defined by the largest blade the machine can handle, not on the power available to drive the blade. I used an 8-inch Sears table saw for a long time, then switched to a 10 inch. The blade in the machine is almost more important than the machine itself. For years I used a hollow-ground planer blade from

Sears; now I use a thin-kerf, carbide-tipped Japanese blade that cuts a kerf only $\frac{1}{16}$ inch thick. A 7 $\frac{1}{4}$-inch blade doesn't overload the saw, creates less sawdust than a larger blade, and saves material.

When ripping strips on a table saw, use a fingerboard to hold the material tightly to the rip fence. I do not use a second fingerboard to push down on the material, however. I usually work by myself, and with a double fingerboard setup, if anything were to bind up, I might be way out on the end of a 16-foot piece of wood, a long way from the switch. With only a single fingerboard pushing in against the fence, I can always free the board I am ripping by lifting up on the end.

Any accident with a table saw is a serious accident. For safety's sake, keep your table saw blade set just high enough to cut all the way through the material and no higher. Anything that makes it more difficult for you to accidentally touch the blade when it is turning is a good thing.

Never use a table saw in poor light, or when you are overtired, which is when most accidents happen. As a matter of policy, when I get overtired I don't do anything but take a nap.

Never use a dull blade. I keep my strip-ripping blades separate from the rest and use them only for ripping strips. They stay sharp longer that way.

Before sawing any lumber with your table saw, check carefully for staples and other fastenings, which can ruin your saw blade. Especially check the ends of the lumber; sometimes the shipper has stapled a red flag there, and the lumberyard crew has pulled off the flag and left the staples.

Random-Orbit Sander

After the table saw, the random orbit sander is the next in importance, followed by the router. I use a Porter Cable 6-inch variable-speed random-orbit sander, model number 7336. (I have tried Porter Cable's smaller random-orbit sander, the 5-inch model, but found it difficult to use and therefore do not recommend it.) I replaced the pad that comes installed on the sander with a contour pad, which is softer and works far better for my canoe work than the original pad. The contour pad uses stick-on discs, which can be obtained at any good autobody store. This sander, with the extra counter pad, costs about $160; it's a good tool and well worth the price. The only problem I have had with it is in the switch, which clogs up with sanding dust and must be cleaned periodically.

I recently bought a new random-orbit sander from Porter Cable, model number 332. It is more like a palm sander, strictly for finish work, and that is why I bought it. It was much cheaper than the 6-incher, and nowhere near as powerful. I wanted something gentle, and that is what I got. It could probably be used to sand an entire boat, but it would take a lot longer than the 6-inch model.

I use a Makita palm sander for finish sanding between coats of varnish. It's a great little tool. I have used it on every canoe I ever built, and have never had any problems with it.

Router

I use a wide variety of routers. Some were leftover from my carpenter days, others were bought specifically for canoe use.

To cove and bead the planking strips, I use a 3-horsepower Sears router made by Ryobi in a router table that I built myself. The feature I like best about it is the ease of adjustment. Without removing the router from its place in the table, I can make small, accurate adjustments. Just reach down under and turn a knob for either up or down a fraction of an inch. Expect to pay at least $200 for a big plunge router like this one. A smaller router will do the job, but adjustment can be a real problem.

A large plunge router is difficult to use freehand, even though most of those available today have a slow-start mechanism, so I use a smaller router when free-handing rails, deck edging, or other material on the boat. It is a $\frac{7}{8}$-horsepower Porter Cable, model number 100. Some routers are very awkward to use, but not this one. It is a fairly light tool, with decent visibility so you can see what the bit is actually doing. The ability to see the cutting edge of any tool adds to the safety factor.

Sabersaw

A sabersaw makes cutting out the molds an easy job. It is also effective for cutting out the laminations for a spoon-bladed paddle. I far prefer the Bosch variable speed, model number 1587 VS, to any other sabersaw I have ever used. In my opinion it is the best planned and engineered sabersaw on the market today. Especially noteworthy is the excellent visibility of the blade as it cuts. Expect to pay about $200 for this machine.

Battery-Powered Drill

A battery-powered combination drill and screwdriver is also a handy tool to have. I use a Panasonic model that is several years old. It's only a 9.5-volt machine but, with two batteries, it more than serves my needs. I use this drill for setting up the molds, to drill and screw the inner rail in place, and to drill the ⅝-inch holes in the bow and stern for the PVC tubes I put in all my canoes for the painters.

Belt Sander

I use a belt sander on the boat itself for only one task — to fair the ends of a canoe to take the outer stem laminations — but I use it off the boat to prepare the rails and seat frames prior to installation. My machine, a Porter Cable I've had for years, takes a 3-inch by 21-inch belt. I use extremely coarse belts (24-grit, almost like sanding with rocks), because they cut fast and don't clog up as quickly as finer belts.

Disc Sander

To rough out the double-paddle blades, I use a Makita sander-polisher, model number 9207spc, priced at around $200. In fourteen years, I haven't found a better tool for this job. It comes in handy for other chores as well. I used to use this tool with a coarse disc to rough sand the exterior and interior of my canoes, but no longer. The coarse disc leaves deep scratches that are difficult to get out with a random-orbit sander. It was too easy to ruin a canoe with a moment's carelessness.

Hand Tools

HAMMER
Anything under 16 ounces is fine.

BLOCK PLANE
This is a very useful tool for fairing the hull prior to sanding, and it must be sharp, as sharp as you can get it. A new one, straight out of the box, isn't sharp enough, so pay special attention to my advice below on sharpening.

CHISELS
You should have at least two, one ⅜ inch, the other ¾ inch. I would rather have one good, sharp chisel than a set of five that won't hold an edge. It pays to buy a quality brand.

TACK PULLER
Use this for pulling staples and nails after the hull is stripped. Most hardware stores carry this tool.

FRAMING SQUARE
For laying out and setting up the molds on the building board.

NYLON CHALKLINE
For putting a centerline on the building board.

STAPLE GUN
I use the Duofast brand, because during over 12 years of use with mine I have never been dissatisfied. This tool is trouble free, easy to operate, and has adjustable power that can control the driving depth of the staple. As it has a soft pull, people who lack a strong grip find it easy to use.

NAIL APRON
To keep your clothes clean and your small tools and fastenings organized. Get one with a hammer holder.

CLAMPS
You can never have too many of them. Probably the two most useful types in building a canoe are small C-clamps and medium-sized (2-inch) spring clamps. I would suggest at least a dozen of each for starters. Several small bar clamps would also be helpful.

Buying all these clamps at one time can be a shock to your pocketbook. I amassed mine by buying two or three clamps every time I went to the lumberyard. If a loved one can be convinced that you would prefer clamps over handkerchiefs for your birthday or Christmas, you will have it made.

SMALL HANDSAW
I use a Dozuki, a Japanese saw that cuts on the pull stroke, with a very fine kerf. American handsaws cut on the push stroke and must be much thicker, thus producing a wide kerf, so as not to crimp when pushed. I prefer the Dozuki that has a very short rib on the back of the saw blade, rather than the extended rib. This makes cutting-in the bottom strips of the boat easier, as I can slide almost the entire blade between the two pieces of wood. These saws are becoming more expensive, but they are well worth the cost; replacement blades are available.

SHARPENING MATERIALS
Entire books have been written about sharpening tools, and the tool catalogs are filled with expensive hard Arkansas stones, Japanese water stones in ten different grits, India stones, carborundum stones, you name it. I now sharpen my chisels and plane irons with inexpensive tools that make getting a good edge simple for anyone: a water-cooled electric wheel from Sears, a honing guide from Veritas, and a piece of glass. The sharpening agents are inexpensive sheets of wet or dry sanding paper, with WD-40 as a lubricant. I use the wet wheel to hollow grind the tool edge, then the honing guide to keep a constant bevel while I refine the edge on sanding paper over glass. I start with a 200-grit paper, then go to 600-grit, and finally a light going over with 1,000-grit. Because the paper is lying flat on the glass, I get a true bevel. I also use the same system to flatten the backs of chisels and plane irons as I go along.

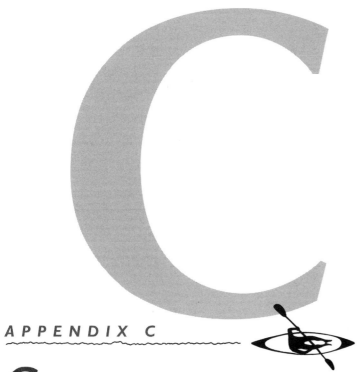

Sources of Supplies

The following is only a small sample of the many companies that supply materials and tools. Try your local suppliers first. If they can't furnish you with quality material, then try these fine companies, many of which advertise in *WoodenBoat* and *Fine Woodworking* magazines, both of which I find fascinating reading (see bibliography). Buying just once from any catalog company will usually bring on a flood of more catalogs from other companies. They all sell their mailing lists to each other, I guess. I find it to be great reading material. If we have to be besieged by junk mail, at least make it tool and boat-supply catalogs, which to my eye have a certain amount of class.

Lumber and Other Materials

BEAR MOUNTAIN BOAT SHOP
275 John St.
Peterborough, ON, Canada, K9J 5E8
705-740-0470
Kits and plans, as well as finished boats.

CLARKCRAFT
16-42 Aqualane
Tonawanda, NY 14150
Patterns, epoxies, wood.

FLOUNDER BAY BOAT LUMBER
1019 3rd Ave.
Anacortes, WA 98221
800-228-4691
Cedar and spruce strips.

THE NEW FOUND WOODWORKS
RR 2 Box 850
Bristol, NH 03222
603-744-6872
Northern white cedar, and Western red-cedar strips, coved and beaded.

ANCHOR HARDWOODS COMPANY
6014-R Oleander Dr.
Wilmington, NC 28403
910-392-9888
Coved and beaded strips in Atlantic white cedar. Also an extensive selection of hardwoods and marine plywood.

TENDER CRAFT BOAT SHOP
311 Markham St.
Toronto, ON, Canada M6G 2K8
416-920-6990
Kits in all degrees of completeness.

There are numerous other companies, both in the U.S. and Canada, that supply materials. The main feature to look for is quality; the second is the freight charge. Sometimes that can be a shocker.

Epoxy & Glass Cloth Suppliers

DEFENDER INDUSTRIES
42 Great Neck Rd.
Waterford, CT 06385
800-628-8225
The only place I know to get 2-ounce cloth for my rowing shells at a fair price. I have had excellent service and materials from them.

GOUGEON BROTHERS
P.O. Box 908
Bay City, MI 48707
517-684-7286
I have been using their West System epoxy and cloth exclusively for the last four years. The only hardener I use is the 207 Special Coating Hardener for a clear finish. Don't use their other hardeners if you want a clear finish. Believe me! One of the reasons I use Gougeon products is their consistent quality; the other is that I can get one-day delivery in this area for any of their products.

SYSTEM THREE RESINS
P.O. Box 70436
Seattle, WA 98107
206-782-7976
I used their materials for a long time and was pleased with the results. I find their wood flour to be the best admixture for color-matching Western red cedar when filling gaps and making repairs.

Plastic Cane and Caning Supplies

H. H. PERKINS
10 S. Bradley Rd.
Woodbridge, CT 06525
203-389-9501
Excellent service and a wide selection of caning and weaving supplies and materials.

Nails

FEATHER CANOES
1705 Andrea Pl.
Sarasota, FL 34235
941-355-6736 or 953-7660
I have a good supply of 1 1/4-inch, No. 18 nails for temporary fastening strips to the molds. Enough to do a couple of canoes is $5, which includes postage, to U.S. addresses.

Tools

WOODCRAFT
800-225-1153
Great catalog, good service, good selection.

HIGHLAND HARDWARE
1045 N. Highland Ave. N.E.
Atlanta, GA 30306
800-241-6748
Another great catalog, good service, good selection.

JAPAN WOODWORKER
1731 Clement Ave.
Alameda, CA 94501
800-537-7820
I buy my Hock plane irons from them. These are of excellent quality and are made in U.S. This company carries a wide selection of tools, many of them American made. Their prices are good, their quality excellent.

THE WOODENBOAT STORE
P.O. Box 78
Brooklin, ME 04616
800-273-SHIP (7447)
Japanese saws and replacement blades.

Router Bits

MLCS
P.O. Box 4053
Rydal, PA 19046
800-533-9298
Sells Taiwanese bits. Much cheaper than elsewhere; quality seems OK.

CMT TOOLS
310 Mears Blvd.
Oldsmar, FL 34677
800-531-5559
High quality router bits and saw blades.

Air Filters

WOODCRAFT
P.O. Box 1686
Parkersburg, WV 26102-1686
800-225-1153

KLINGSPOR'S SANDING CATALOG
P.O. Box 3737
Hickory, NC 28603-3737
800-228-0000

PENN STATE INDUSTRIES
2850 Conley Rd.
Philadelphia, PA 19154
800-377-7297

APPENDIX D

Patterns for the Wee Lassie

The little Wee Lassie that I use as the principal project in this book is quite different from the original Wee Lassie built by J. Henry Rushton back in the 19th century. The original was symmetrical and almost flat bottomed. Actually, the only real similarity between the two is that they would both fit in the same box.

My first contact with the Wee Lassie-type canoe came when I read *Rushton and His Times in American Canoeing,* by Atwood Manley. I had read about the book years ago in the late John Gardner's column in *National Fisherman.* (John Gardner was, and still is, a great influence on my life. When I first started building boats, he and Howard Chapelle were almost the only ones offering information on our rich wooden craft tradition.) In the book was a photograph of the Wee Lassie, and it really turned me on. This canoe — small, light, and simple — was just what I wanted. I knew I had to build one, but the table of offsets —the list of dimensions used to define the lines of the hull—was atrocious. I ended up with a boat that was quite different from the original, but I was on my way. I kept changing the shape of the molds, and their spacing, until I arrived at what I believed was a really neat little double-paddle canoe. I had no way of telling until just recently how far I had wandered from the original.

Since *Rushton and His Times* was published, The Adirondack Museum in Blue Mountain Lake, New York, which owns the original Wee Lassie canoe, had a new, accurate set of lines and offsets prepared. I picked up a set of these plans, laid out the lines and molds according to the dimensions provided in the table of offsets, and superimposed them on the lines and molds for my version. I was surprised by the difference.

The design I build has a longer entrance; i.e., the widest and fullest section (mold) is aft of the centerline. It's that way because I feel it takes more effort to part the water with the bow than to get rid of it at the stern.

The stern molds are a little fuller than those ahead of the middle of the boat. The stern of a canoe being paddled hard in shallow water tends to be sucked down, which causes a drop in speed. This makes you work harder and can make quite a bit of difference when paddling upstream against a current or tide. A fullness aft means the stern is less likely to be sucked down.

The rocker (fore-and-aft curvature of the bottom) in my design is more than that of the original Wee Lassie, which makes the canoe a bit easier to turn.

My design is a shallow V on the bottom, rather than being almost flat. This provides good tracking ability for a short boat, and good lateral stability. She goes where you point her and is remarkably resistant to wind pressure.

Rushton's original design probably had more initial stability than my version, but once it leaned over it would tend to keep on going over farther. My design, with its narrower waterline but flared sides, tends to resist rolling over. Several freestyle paddlers who have used my Wee Lassie complain that it won't roll down to the rail and stay there — it fights to get back upright. They look at this as a fault. I look at it as a blessing. I haven't dunked a camera yet.

This brings up an often-asked question: Why don't you use a keel? Wouldn't that make the boat more stable?

I don't like external keels on a canoe. A shallow-V hull shape resists sideward wind pressure much better than does a keel on a flat-bottomed canoe. A flat-bottomed canoe without a keel would be all over the place most of the time and uncontrollable under some conditions, yet an external keel can cause real problems in exploring the areas I often paddle that are filled with shallow stumps and logs. In tannic-stained water, or water covered with duckweed, you can't see the stumps. A keel will hang up and tilt you over, while a shallow-V-shaped hull without a keel will slide off to the side with a gentle motion. If an external keel gets damaged it will soon let water into the wood of the hull through loosened screws. This you do not want, and usually will not notice until the damage is done. I believe that a barrier coat on the bottom of your canoe is far better for resisting scratches and digs than an outer keel.

The Patterns

Included here are measured drawings of building patterns for the Wee Lassie and the Wee Lassie Two. The latter is similar to my standard design, but it is for a 13-foot, 6-inch long hull. It is ideal for the heavier or taller user, or for someone who would prefer a longer canoe to carry more camping gear. The Wee Lassie Two is not designed to carry two adults — only one — and it is not just a stretched-out version of the Wee Lassie. Rather, it is a completely different boat that paddles very well.

By the way, I have received quite a few letters from people who have radically altered the Wee Lassie (the usual change is to stretch the hull way out). Personally, I like it just the way it is.

The measured drawings included here are used for laying out the patterns full-size. This is how it works:

On a piece of poster board, use a framing square to lay out a grid of lines one inch apart. Let one side edge of the poster board represent the centerline of the hull, and the bottom edge represent the top of the building board.

Using a ruler, at each line measure out from the centerline the correct number of inches and fractions and make a mark. When you have a mark on each line, all you have to do is connect the marks with a thin, flexible batten, and cut out the full-size pattern. Now lay the poster-board pattern onto the plywood or particle board that you will be using for the molds and trace around it.

Note that the measured drawings show one-half of the full-size mold patterns. To get the other half, flip the pattern over, using the centerline for alignment.

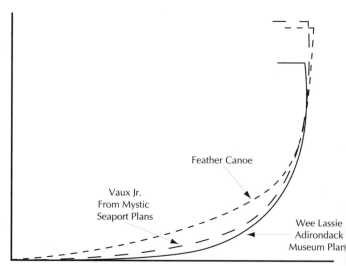

A comparison of mid-sections.

If you do not want to go to the trouble of laying out the patterns for the boat full-size, you can save all of this bother by ordering full-size patterns from me. My full-size patterns have been used by hundreds of amateur builders with great results.

Ordering Full-Size Patterns

Full-size patterns at $20 per set are available for the Wee Lassie, the Wee Lassie Two, and the Feather Sailing Canoe. I also have full-size patterns for two tandem canoes, a rowing shell, a guideboat, and the melonseed sailboat. To order these patterns, or for more information:

Mac McCarthy
Feather Canoes
1705 Andrea Pl.
Sarasota, FL 34235
941-355-6736, 941-953-7660

Patterns for the Wee Lassie Canoe

ALL PATTERN DRAWINGS: THOMAS MCCARTHY

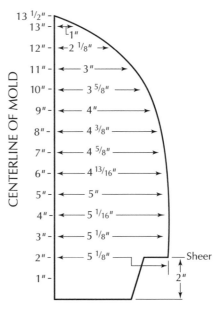

Mold #1
(Not to scale)

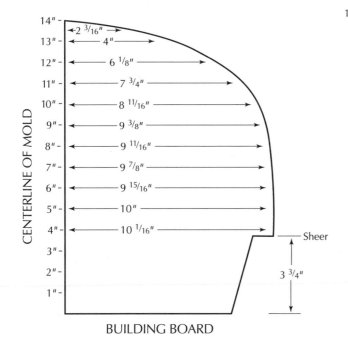

Mold #2
(Not to scale)

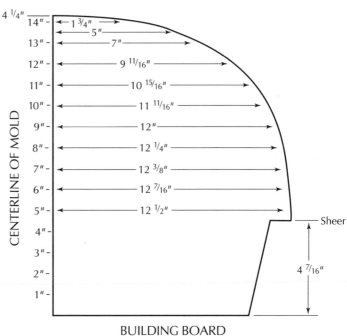

Mold #3
(Not to scale)

Patterns for the Wee Lassie Canoe

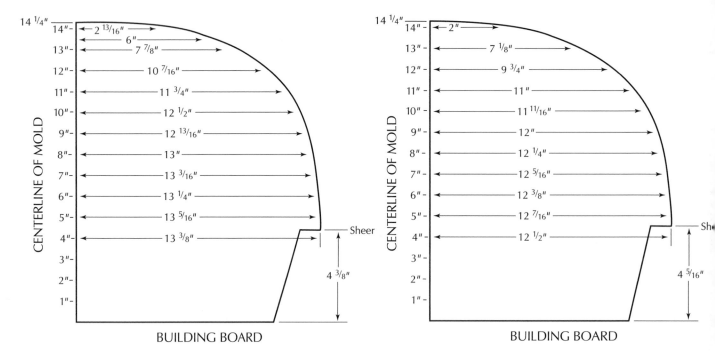

Mold #4
(Not to scale)

Mold #5
(Not to scale)

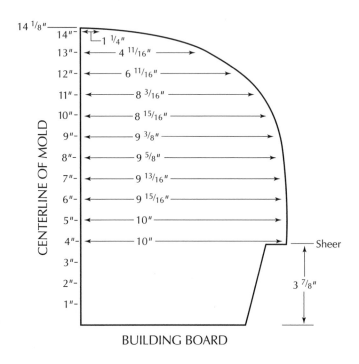

Mold #6
(Not to scale)

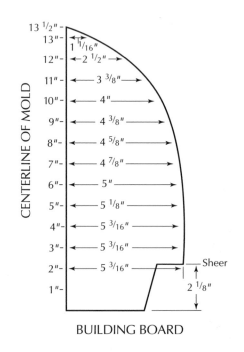

Mold #7
(Not to scale)

Patterns for the Wee Lassie Canoe

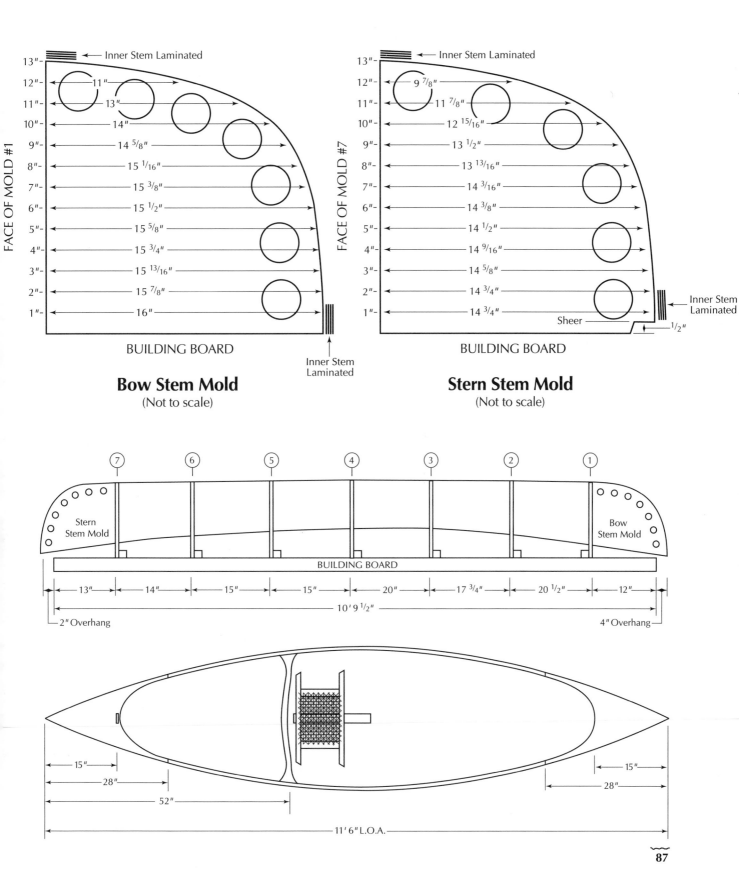

FACE OF MOLD #1

13" ← Inner Stem Laminated
12" — 11"
11" — 13"
10" — 14"
9" — 14 5/8"
8" — 15 1/16"
7" — 15 3/8"
6" — 15 1/2"
5" — 15 5/8"
4" — 15 3/4"
3" — 15 13/16"
2" — 15 7/8"
1" — 16"

BUILDING BOARD

Inner Stem Laminated

Bow Stem Mold
(Not to scale)

FACE OF MOLD #7

13" ← Inner Stem Laminated
12" — 9 7/8"
11" — 11 7/8"
10" — 12 15/16"
9" — 13 1/2"
8" — 13 13/16"
7" — 14 3/16"
6" — 14 3/8"
5" — 14 1/2"
4" — 14 9/16"
3" — 14 5/8"
2" — 14 3/4"
1" — 14 3/4"
Sheer — 1/2"

Inner Stem Laminated

Stern Stem Mold
(Not to scale)

⑦ ⑥ ⑤ ④ ③ ② ①

Stern Stem Mold   Bow Stem Mold

BUILDING BOARD

| 13" | 14" | 15" | 15" | 20" | 17 3/4" | 20 1/2" | 12" |

10'9 1/2"

2" Overhang   4" Overhang

15"   15"
28"   28"
52"
11'6" L.O.A.

Patterns for the Wee Lassie Two

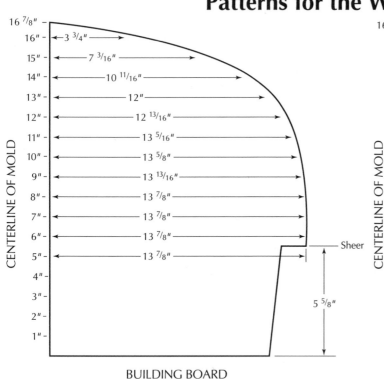

Mold #1 – Need One
(Not to scale)

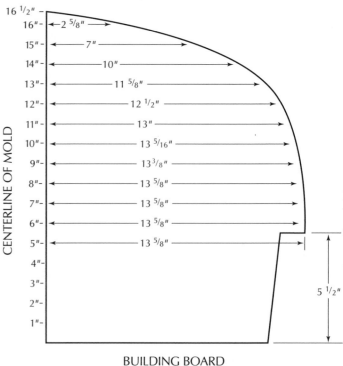

Mold #2 – Need Two
(Not to scale)

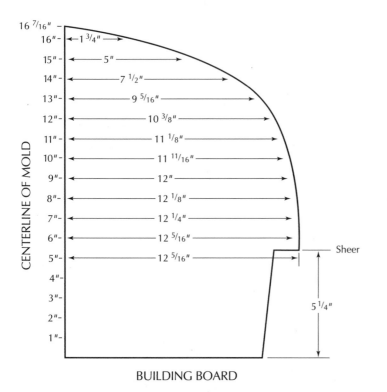

Mold #3 – Need Two
(Not to scale)

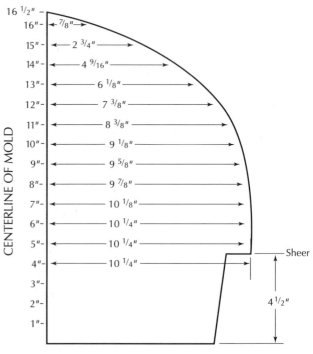

Mold #4 – Need Two
(Not to scale)

Patterns for the Wee Lassie Two

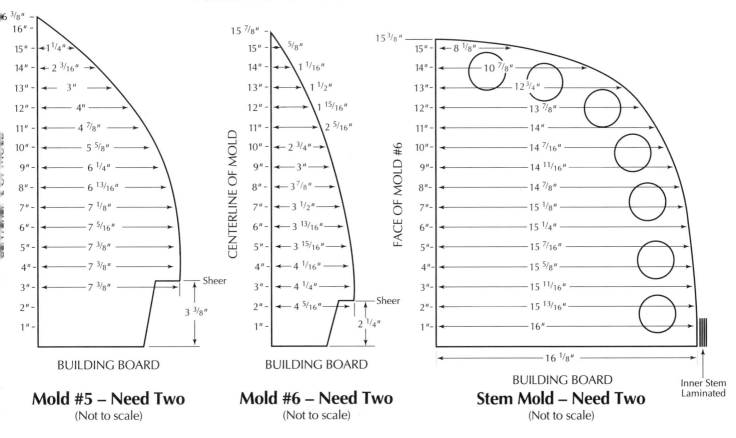

Mold #5 – Need Two
(Not to scale)

Mold #6 – Need Two
(Not to scale)

Stem Mold – Need Two
(Not to scale)

Inner Stem
Laminated

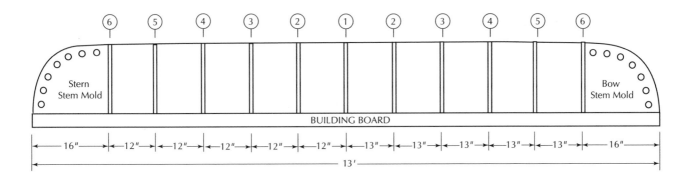

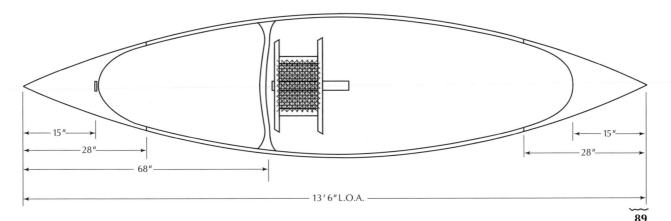

BIBLIOGRAPHY

When I first started building cedar strip canoes there was very little literature on classic small craft of any type. This situation has greatly improved in the last few years. Here is an annotated list of books and articles that have guided me along the way and that should be useful to you.

Books

An Adirondack Passage, by Christine Jerome. Harper Collins, New York, 1995.
> A cruising story and historical commentary; compares the 1800s with the present day. Makes good reading before traveling the same route.

American Small Sailing Craft, by Howard I. Chapelle. W.W. Norton, New York, 1951.
> There are some wonderful boats to build in this book. I bought my copy back in 1951 and must have read it a thousand times. Still in print.

The Bark Canoes and Skin Boats of North America, by Edwin Tappan Adney and Howard I. Chapelle. Smithsonian Institution, Washington, D.C., 1964.
> An excellent reference. Many interesting designs, both canoes and kayaks.

Boats, Oars and Rowing, by R. D. "Pete" Culler. International Marine Publishing Co., Camden, Maine, 1978.
> This is a real jewel, a small book loaded with common sense. Good section on double-paddle canoes.

Building Classic Small Craft, Vol. 2, by John Gardner. International Marine Publishing Co., Camden, Maine, 1984.

Contains an entire chapter on classic canoes, with several canoe tables of offsets.

Many of John Gardner's articles in the monthly *National Fisherman* newspaper over the years contain helpful suggestions about canoe building. His writing was an inspiration to me when I was first getting into canoe building.

Canoe and Boat Building for Amateurs, by W.P. Stephens. Forest and Stream, New York, 1885.

Long out of print but sometimes available in rare-book stores. Reproductions of the fold-out plates of plans for classic decked sailing canoes that originally came with this book are available from Mystic Seaport Museum.

Canoes and Canoeing, by Percy Blandford. Lutterworth Press, London, 1962.

Mostly about wood-frame, fabric-covered, kayak-style boats, but still interesting.

Canoecraft, by Ted Moores and Merilyn Mohr. Camden House Publishing, Camden East, ON, Canada, 1983.

Practical book on modern cedar-strip canoe building. Includes plans for tandem canoes.

Canoeing the Adirondacks with Nessmuk, by George Washington Sears. The Adirondack Museum/ Syracuse University Press, Blue Mountain Lake, New York, 1995.

Discusses the versatility of the open double-paddle canoe; see also *Woodcraft and Camping*.

The Compleat Cruiser, by L. Francis Herreshoff. Sheridan House, New York, 1987.

Chapter and opinions on the decked double-paddle canoe, plus a sketch of a Rob Roy-type canoe.

Pete Culler's Boats, by John Burke. International Marine Publishing Co., Camden, Maine, 1984.

Contains plans for several double-paddle canoes, as well as many fine sailing and rowing boats.

On the River, edited by Walter Magnes Teller. Rutgers University Press, New Jersey, 1976

Stories about cruising in canoes, including many of the double-paddle type.

Rushton and His Times in American Canoeing, by Atwood Manley. The Adirondack Museum/Syracuse University Press, New York, 1968.

Good information but poor tables of offsets for six of Rushton's designs. These tables of offsets, as incomplete as they are, were the jumping off place for many builders, myself included.

Sail and Oar, by John Leather. International Marine Publishing Co., Camden, Maine, 1982.

Chapter on double-paddle canoes.

Woodcraft and Camping, by "Nessmuk" (George Washington Sears), first published in 1884, reprinted by Dover Publications.

Where-to-Go Guides

The following guidebooks are well done and typical of the type. They list put-in and take-out spots, the difficulties of the waterways, and the type of scenery. In most, you have to learn to read between the lines. These books will give you an idea of the tremendous variety of streams and rivers you can paddle your little canoe on. They are mainly limited to the U.S. East Coast, the only area where I have so far had the opportunity to do much canoeing. There are books similar to these for just about any area in the U.S. that you would want to canoe.

Planning ahead can prevent the wasting of time on a trip. You don't want to go out of your way driving to a stream that doesn't have water in it at that particular time of year. Neither do you want to discover when it's too late that you need a four-wheel-drive truck to reach that perfect spot, while you only have a low-powered, four-cylinder caravan.

I find guidebooks about rivers and streams a pleasure to read; they induce daydreams about paddling all of them.

I might also mention that I have discovered many great places to canoe by casually reading various magazines, among them *Audubon, Sierra, Outside*, and many others.

Adirondack Canoe Waters, North Flow, by Jamieson and Morris. 1988. Adirondack Mountain Club, RR 3, Box 3055, Lake George, NY 12845.

Adventuring Along the Gulf of Mexico, by Donald Schueler. 1986. Sierra Club, 730 Polk St., San Francisco, CA 94109.

Describes rivers, streams, and campgrounds from

the Florida Keys up the west coast, and across the panhandle to Alabama, Mississippi, Louisiana, Texas, and beyond. An excellent guidebook.

AMC Quiet Water Canoe Guide: Maine. 1995. Appalachian Mountain Club Books, 5 Joy St., Boston, MA 02108.

AMC Quiet Water Canoe Guide: New Hampshire and Vermont, by Alex Wilson. 1992. Appalachian Mountain Club Books, 5 Joy St., Boston, MA 02108.

Canoeing and Kayaking Guide to the Streams of Florida, Volumes One and Two. Menasha Ridge Press, 3169 Cahaba Heights Rd., Birmingham, AL 35243.

Canoe Trails of the Deep South, by Estes, Carter, and Almquist. 1991. Menasha Ridge Press, 3169 Cahaba Heights Rd., Birmingham, AL 35243.
   A typical paddler's guide to Alabama, Missisippi, and Louisiana.

Exploring The Little Rivers of New Jersey, by James and Margaret Cawley. 1993. Rutgers University Press, New Brunswick, NJ 08901.

Maryland and Delaware Canoe Trails, by Edward Gertler. 1983. Senaca Press, Silver Spring, MD.

Paddling South Carolina, by Abel and Horan. 1990. Sandlapper Publishing Company, Orangeburg, SC.

Paddlers Guide to Eastern North Carolina, by Benner and McCloud. 1991. Menasha Ridge Press, 3169 Cahaba Heights Rd., Birmingham, AL 35243

Southern Georgia Canoeing, by Schlinger and Otey. 1980. Menasha Ridge Press, 3169 Cahaba Heights Rd., Birmingham, AL 35243.

Magazines

Backpacker, Rodale Press, Inc., 33 E. Minor St., Emmaus, PA 18098
   Has good articles on quiet-water canoeing and places to go as well as on camping gear, most of which relate directly to canoe camping.

Boat Design Quarterly. Available from Wooden-Boat Store, P.O. Box 78, Brooklin, ME 04616.
   Often has designs of double-paddle canoes, as well as many other interesting boats.

Canoe and Kayak, 10526 N. E. 68th, Suite 3, Kirkland, WA 98033.
   I find this magazine hardly worth reading. Mostly about whitewater paddling.

Fine Woodworking, P.O. Box 5507, Newtown, CT 06470-9871

Messing About in Boats, 29 Burley St., Wenham, MA 01984-1943.
   This neat little magazine comes out every two weeks and covers the entire small boating scene. Many interesting articles on paddling, rowing, and sailing all types of small boats. Advertisements for specialized hardware and materials, plus many classified ads for used small boats and equipment.

Sea Kayaker, 7001 Seaview Ave. NW, Suite 135, Seattle, WA 98117-6059.
   While totally devoted to sea kayaking, this magazine has great articles on paddling technique and equipment that also apply to the small double-paddle type open canoe.

WoodenBoat, P.O. Box 78, Brooklin, ME 04616.
   Excellent magazine for anyone who is interested in wooden boats, traditional or modern. Contains advertisements for canoe plans and canoe-building materials, plus many articles on wooden canoes in general. Back issues with these articles are available.

Wooden Canoe, the journal of the Wooden Canoe Heritage Association, P.O. Box 226, Blue Mountain Lake, NY 12812.
   A first-class magazine totally devoted to wooden canoes, their history and restoration. Over the years they have published several of my articles about small double-paddle canoes. If you have a wooden canoe, you really should belong to the association, which has a great assembly each year.

INTERESTING INDIVIDUAL MAGAZINE ARTICLES
Rudder, February, 1948.
   Article by L. Francis Herreshoff on double paddles, backrests, etc.

Rudder, January and November, 1954.
Articles by Commander Beebe, experiments with double-paddle canoes, building methods, and designs. I was avidly reading these articles long before I had the skills to build boats like these.

Rudder, November, 1954
The canoe Boris, with a table of offsets. I built the Boris in cedar strip about 14 years ago and enjoyed paddling it for a year or more before I sold it. A decked, double-paddle canoe, she was stable enough to stand up in.

Small Boat Journal, Vol. 1, No. 7
An article about a take-apart Wee Lassie.

Small Boat Journal, Vol. 1, No. 9.
The article by Carol Storrs on the small, light-weight, double-paddle canoe was instrumental in getting me interested in the type.

WoodenBoat, issue no. 90
An article by Mike O'Brien on double-paddle canoes.

WoodenBoat, issue no. 100
An article by me on how to build the Wee Lassie, step-by-step.

WoodenBoat, issue no. 100
Article by Peter H. Spectre on a double-paddle canoe trip in the Adirondacks.

If you can locate back issues of *CanoeSport* magazine, you will discover some excellent articles on paddling technique and quiet-water paddling. The same applies to back issues of *Small Boat Journal*, the further back the better. Before *SBJ* was trashed, it had superb coverage of small rowing and sailing craft, as well as canoes and paddling.

Sources of Plans and Books
The Adirondack Museum, P.O. Box 99, Blue Mountain Lake, NY 12812. 518-352-7311.
Canoe plans, books about canoeing, and the history and geography of the Adirondack area.

Mystic Seaport Museum, P.O. Box 6000 Mystic, CT 06335-0990.
Plans and books, and the site of many boat shows and get-togethers. Plan on a full day if you visit.

Smithsonian Institution, Div. of Trans. Washington, D.C., 20560
An exceptional source for plans, including the plates from Howard I. Chapelle's books. Getting these plans allows you to read the tables of offsets without a magnifying glass. Some of these boats can be built with this system. Fishing schooners, Chinese junks, Civil War blockade-runners, as well as canoes and kayaks. The variety is endless.

Boatbuilding Books from

How to Build the Shellback Dinghy
by Eric Dow

Construct a beautiful dinghy following the step-by-step instructions of builder Eric Dow. The Shellback Dinghy is a modern classic with a traditional bow, a narrow rockered bottom, and a sweet transom that lifts well out of the water. Engineered with the amateur builder in mind, the Shellback has a practically frameless interior (there's a single laminated 'midship frame), which also makes her easy to clean and paint. The glued-lapstrake construction means she won't dry out when stored out of water for long periods of time.
Product #325-040
64 pp., illus., softcover
$15.00

How to Build the Haven 12 ½-Footer
by Maynard Bray

Developed by Joel White for a client who loved the Herreshoff 12½ but required a shallow draft, the Haven 12½ is a keel/centerboard variation of the original. This book will show you how to construct her using the same process used to build the original Herreshoffs in Bristol, Rhode Island. She's built upside down, with a mold for every frame. No lofting is required. Each step in this unique process is carefully explained and illustrated, which, with detailed construction plans (not included), provides a thorough guide for advanced amateurs.
Product #325-077
64 pp., illus., softcover
$15.00

Building the Nutshell Pram
by Maynard Bray

A step-by-step manual for the construction of this very popular Joel White design, for oar and sail. This revised instruction book is beneficial for anyone who wishes to build the pram from scratch using WoodenBoat's full-scale plans. Includes a listing of tools, materials, and fastenings, and more than 100 step-by-step photographs. Describes setting up, building, and fitting out the hull; constructing and installing the daggerboard trunk; making the rudder; rigging the pram for sail; and sailing techniques.
Product #325-035
32 pp., illus., softcover
$7.95

How to Build the Catspaw Dinghy:
A Boat for Oar and Sail
by the Editors of WoodenBoat

A detailed manual on the building of a superior rowing and sailing dinghy. A modified version of the famous Herreshoff Columbia model dinghy, this boat, which measures 12' 8", makes an excellent project for the boatbuilder with intermediate skills. It is fitted with a centerboard and a simple sprit rig, and is built carvel style over steam-bent frames. The boat can be built right out of this guide (although using the plans is recommended), which contains carefully illustrated step-by-step building instructions, and reduced lines, offsets, construction plan, and sail plan.
Product #325-010
32 pp., illus., softcover
$8.95

WoodenBoat Publications

Forty Wooden Boats
by the Editors of WoodenBoat

Our study plans catalogs are best-sellers because they allow you to compare and contrast a variety of designs and building techniques along with providing vital statistics. Information includes beam, length, sail area, suggested engine, alternative construction methods, skill level needed (ranked by beginner, intermediate or advanced builder), level of detail provided in each plan, plus thought-provoking commentary.

Some of the 40 designs include L. Francis Herreshoff's ROZINANTE, Brewer's Mystic Sharpie, 5 kayaks built in a variety of methods (including a double-kayak), a canoe, 2 peapods (one of traditional plank-on-frame construction, the other glued-lap plywood), a catamaran, daysailers, a single and double rowing shell, skiffs, mahogany runabouts from the boards of Nelson Zimmer and Ken Bassett, and many more. The reader will find a tremendous amount of information at their fingertips at a very low price. These are the newest designs added to WoodenBoat's collection since the publication of *Fifty Wooden Boats* and *Thirty Wooden Boats*.
Product #325-062
96 pp., illus., softcover
$12.95

Fifty Wooden Boats
by the Editors of WoodenBoat

This popular book contains details usually found with study plans: hull dimensions, displacement, sail area, construction methods, and the degree of boatbuilding skill needed to complete each project. Along with the 50 designs—which range from a 7′ 7″ pram to a 41′3″ schooner— there are drawings that identify the parts of a wooden boat, a bibliography, a guide for the selection of various woods, and instructions by Weston Farmer on reading boat plans. Unlike most plans catalogs, *Fifty Wooden Boats* also contains lines that let you see the hulls' shapes.
Product #325-060
112 pp., illus., softcover
$12.95

Thirty Wooden Boats
by the Editors of WoodenBoat

More study plans selected by the Editors of *WoodenBoat*. This volume describes the designs that were added to our collection after the publication of *Fifty Wooden Boats*.

These 30 designs include: 6 powerboats, 6 daysailers, 11 cruising boats, 2 canoes, a kayak, and 4 small sailing/pulling boats. Also included is an article by designer Joel White on understanding boat plans.
Product #325-061
80 pp., illus., softcover
$12.95

The WoodenBoat Store
P.O. Box 78 • Brooklin, ME 04616-0078
Call Toll-Free U.S. & Canada: 1–800–273–SHIP (7447)

The WoodenBoat Store

P.O. Box 78, Naskeag Road, Brooklin, Maine 04616-0078

EMail: wbstore@woodenboat.com

Toll-Free U.S. & Canada:
1-800-273-SHIP (7447)

Hours: 8am–6pm EST, Mon.–Fri. (9–5 Sats. Oct.–Dec.)
24-Hour Fax: 207-359-8920 **Overseas:** Call 207-359-4647
Internet Address: http://www.woodenboat.com

Ordered by _____

Address _____

City/State/Zip _____

Day Phone# _____

| Catalog Code | **WPB** |

SHIP TO — only if different than "ORDERED BY"

Name _____

Address _____

_____

City/State/Zip _____

Product #	Qty.	Item, Size, Color	Ship Wt.	Total

WoodenBoat Magazine—US Subscriptions: One-year $27.00, Two-years $51.00, Three-years $75.00

Our Guarantee... Satisfaction or Your Money Back!

SUB TOTAL	
Maine Residents Add 6% Tax	
❑ Standard / ❑ Priority Mail	
❑ Two Day / ❑ Next Day	
❑ Int'l Surface / ❑ Int'l Air	
TOTAL	

Pre-payment is required. Payment MUST be in U.S. funds payable on a U.S. bank,

VISA **VISA**   MasterCard **MasterCard**   Discover **DISCOVER**   Check, or Money Orders.

CARD NUMBER												EXPIRES Month/Year (required)	
SIGNATURE OF CARDHOLDER													

U.S. Shipping Charges

	Standard Delivery		Priority Mail		Rush Delivery	
Zip Codes up to 49999	49999	50000+	49999	50000	Two Day	Next Day
Minimum	$2.00	$2.00	$3.00	$3.00	$7.50	$12.00
½ to 1 lb.	3.00	3.00	3.00	3.00	7.50	13.50
up to 2 lbs.	3.00	3.00	3.00	3.00	8.50	14.50
up to 5 lbs.	4.50	6.00	6.50	6.50	9.50	18.50
up to 10 lbs	5.00	8.00	10.00	14.50	15.50	26.00
up to 15 lbs	6.00	10.00	14.00	20.00	21.50	31.50
Add for each additional 5 lbs.	+1.00	+2.00	+5.00	+5.00	+5.00	+5.00

Alaska and Hawaii ADD $10.00 to Two Day and Next Day Charges (No PO Boxes.)

International Shipping

CANADIAN CHARGES	OVERSEAS SURFACE	OVERSEAS PRIORITY/AIR
Up to 1/2 lb. $3.00	Up to 1/2 lb. $4.00	Up to 1/2 lb. $7.00
Up to 2 lbs. 5.00	Up to 2 lbs. 9.00	Up to 1 lbs. 13.00
Up to 3 lbs. 6.50	Up to 3 lbs. 11.00	Up to 2 lbs. 22.00
Up to 4 lbs. 8.00	Up to 4 lbs. 13.00	Up to 3 lbs. 28.00
		Up to 4 lbs. 34.00
ADD $1.50 for each additional lb. PRIORITY/AIR: ADD $2.00 to Total	ADD $2.00 for each additional lb. (Allow 2-4 months for delivery)	ADD $6.00 for each additional lb. (Allow 2-4 weeks)

The WoodenBoat Store

P.O. Box 78, Naskeag Road, Brooklin, Maine 04616-0078

EMail: wbstore@woodenboat.com

Toll-Free U.S. & Canada:
1-800-273-SHIP (7447)

Hours: 8am–6pm EST, Mon.–Fri. (9–5 Sats. Oct.–Dec.)
24-Hour Fax: 207-359-8920 **Overseas:** Call 207-359-4647
Internet Address: http://www.woodenboat.com

Ordered by _____

Address _____

_____

City/State/Zip _____

Day Phone# _____

Catalog Code **WPB**

SHIP TO — only if different than "ORDERED BY"

Name _____

Address _____

_____

City/State/Zip _____

Product #	Qty.	Item, Size, Color	Ship Wt.	Total

WoodenBoat Magazine—US Subscriptions: One-year $27.00, Two-years $51.00, Three-years $75.00

Our Guarantee... Satisfaction or Your Money Back!

Pre-payment is required. Payment MUST be in U.S. funds payable on a U.S. bank,
VISA **VISA**   MasterCard **MasterCard**   Discover **DISCOVER**   Check, or Money Orders.

CARD NUMBER

SIGNATURE OF CARDHOLDER

EXPIRES Month/Year (required)

	Total
SUB TOTAL	
Maine Residents Add 6% Tax	
❑ Standard ❑ Priority Mail	
❑ Two Day ❑ Next Day	
❑ Int'l Surface ❑ Int'l Air	
TOTAL	

U.S. Shipping Charges

	Standard Delivery		Priority Mail		Rush Delivery	
Zip Codes up to 49999	50000+		49999	50000	Two Day	Next Day
Minimum	$2.00	$2.00	$3.00	$3.00	$7.50	$12.00
½ to 1 lb.	3.00	3.00	3.00	3.00	7.50	13.50
up to 2 lbs.	3.00	3.00	3.00	3.00	8.50	14.50
up to 5 lbs.	4.50	6.00	6.50	6.50	9.50	18.50
up to 10 lbs	5.00	8.00	10.00	14.50	15.50	26.00
up to 15 lbs	6.00	10.00	14.00	20.00	21.50	31.50
Add for each additional 5 lbs.	+1.00	+2.00	+5.00	+5.00	+5.00	+5.00

Alaska and Hawaii ADD $10.00 to Two Day and Next Day Charges (No PO Boxes.)

International Shipping

CANADIAN CHARGES	OVERSEAS SURFACE	OVERSEAS PRIORITY/AIR
Up to 1/2 lb. $3.00	Up to 1/2 lb. $4.00	Up to 1/2 lb. $7.00
Up to 2 lbs. 5.00	Up to 2 lbs. 9.00	Up to 1 lbs. 13.00
Up to 3 lbs. 6.50	Up to 3 lbs. 11.00	Up to 2 lbs. 22.00
Up to 4 lbs. 8.00	Up to 4 lbs. 13.00	Up to 3 lbs. 28.00
		Up to 4 lbs. 34.00
ADD $1.50 for each additional lb. PRIORITY/AIR: ADD $2.00 to Total	ADD $2.00 for each additional lb. (Allow 2-4 months for delivery)	ADD $6.00 for each additional lb. (Allow 2-4 weeks)